ENGLAND IN THE 1880s

OLD GUARD AND AVANT-GARDE

England in the 1880s

Old Guard and Avant-Garde

MARGARET D. STETZ
and
MARK SAMUELS LASNER

With an Introduction by
JEROME HAMILTON BUCKLEY

UNIVERSITY PRESS OF VIRGINIA
Charlottesville

Z
2013
.S73
1989

THE UNIVERSITY PRESS OF VIRGINIA
Copyright © 1989 by the Rector and Visitors
of the University of Virginia

First published 1989

LIBRARY OF CONGRESS
Library of Congress Cataloging-in-Publication Data
Stetz, Margaret D. (Margaret Diane), 1953–
England in the 1880s : old guard and avant-garde / Margaret D.
Stetz and Mark Samuels Lasner : with an introduction by Jerome
Hamilton Buckley.
p. cm.
Catalog of an exhibition held at the University of Virginia
Library Feb. 2—Mar. 31, 1985.
Includes index.
ISBN 0–8139–1137–0 (pbk.) : $30.00
1. English literature—19th century—Bibliography—Exhibitions.
2. Literature, Experimental—England—Bibliography—Exhibitions.
3. Avant-garde (Aesthetics)—England—Exhibitions. 4. England—
Intellectual life—19th century—Exhibitions. I. Samuels Lasner,
Mark. II. University of Virginia. Library. III. Title.
Z2013.S73 1989
[PR461]
016.82'08'008—dc19   88-15394
                                                              CIP

Printed in the United States of America

To
SIMON NOWELL SMITH

�za CONTENTS �za

✻ PREFACE ✻

In 1930, when several of the Fellows of the Royal Society of Literature gathered together their essays on the 1880s in a volume under
the editorship of Walter de la Mare, theirs was as much a project of
critical reclamation as of scholarship. Two decades of rabid anti-
Victorian sentiment had turned the major names of the late nineteenth century, old guard and avant-garde alike, from household
words into household jokes. And the pressure of an age of cynicism
was hard to resist. Even some of those contributors to the volume
who began in a spirit of generosity ended by diminishing, if not
vilifying, their predecessors. Thus, Forrest Reid, in the piece called
"Minor Fiction in the 'Eighties," assured his contemporaries that
Olive Schreiner's *The Story of an African Farm* (1883) was "not a
book to be re-read. If we have read it and cared for it in the old days,
it will be wiser to leave it at that," while T. S. Eliot, in determining
"The Place of Pater," managed to assign him a lowly and inconse-
quential one:

> I have spoken of the book [Walter Pater's *Marius the Epicurean*] as
> of some importance. I do not mean that its importance is due to any
> influence it may have exerted. I do not believe that Pater, in this book,
> has influenced a single first-rate mind of a later generation. His view
> of art, as expressed in *The Renaissance*, impressed itself upon a
> number of writers in the 'nineties, and propagated some confusion
> between life and art which is not wholly irresponsible for some untidy
> lives. The theory (if it can be called a theory) of 'art for art's sake' is
> still valid in so far as it can be taken as an exhortation to the artist to
> stick to his job; it never was and never can be valid for the spectator,
> reader or auditor.[1]

Yet beneath the collective raised eyebrows lay signs of a different
expression and of a very different estimate of the late Victorians.

Walter de la Mare captured this mood in his introduction, as he pointed readers toward another way of seeing the past by juxtaposing it with the present: "The Nineteen-Twenties have gone their way. The Nineteen-Eighties—and into what a markless azure vacuum the phrase transports us—will enjoy a far clearer view of their literary achievement than is practicable now. Still, for bare comparison of the last ten years with a decade that is gone indeed, and as an occasion perhaps for a brief pause in our self-congratulations, even the confused catalogue that follows may be of service."[2] His "confused catalogue" was a long list of titles of books written by over thirty philosophers, novelists, poets, and historians, all published in the 1880s and still widely read and admired by de la Mare's contemporaries. By implication, it was the earlier decade that had proved the more fertile, more industrious, and more brilliant and that would "impress itself" more strongly upon the "markless azure vacuum" of future critical opinion. The post–World War I generation had failed to match the abundance and creative force of the generation at which it was inclined to sneer; the parents and grandparents still outshone the children.

Looking back now through the lens of not fifty but one hundred years and across the distance of an ocean, we no longer feel the need to choose between these two decades or to measure them against each other. Neither are we moved to define the character of our own day through opposition to the Victorian age. In compiling this record of an exhibition, what we have aimed at is a fair and comprehensive summary of an intellectually and artistically vigorous period about which there is still much to learn. But inevitably, we have fallen away at moments from this objective spirit of inquiry and been seduced by our subject matter into producing a sort of celebration of the times. It is hard not to slip into a mood of nostalgia, almost of envy, in the face of the tremendous confidence displayed by each and every figure of the 1880s represented here—confidence in deserving, finding, and reaching an audience. Whether a conservative or a revolutionary, a member of what we have called the mid-Victorian old guard or of the fin-de-siècle avant-garde, and whether essayist or biologist, poet or potter, each woman and man who made a public statement appears to have believed that it would carry and reverberate, if not to the many then certainly to the worthy few. Surely it was no coincidence that this was the last age in England when the audience for all forms of culture—whether scientific, visual, or literary—was so homogeneous in class and background, although so divided in its opinions. The creator knew unerringly the language, assumptions, and prejudices of the reader or viewer, even when he or she did not approve of them. This knowledge gave the writer or artist of the 1880s a power, rarely felt since, of playing with perfect assurance upon the audience as on an instrument, of moving it with ease to surrender the desired note, whether one of assent or of anger and surprise. Indeed, as Oscar Wilde proved in the early 1880s before his literary achievements had caught up with his reputation, one could found a career upon such knowledge alone.

But unlike the women and men of the 1880s, we send our work into something of a void, and we must ask ourselves anxiously for whom this volume is intended and to whom it will be of use. Certainly its primary appeal will be to those who are building collections, either for university and public libraries or for themselves. It began with an exhibition designed to highlight a collection—the late nineteenth-century British holdings of the Rare Books Department of the University of Virginia Library—but rapidly expanded to highlight the accomplishments in many fields of this particularly exciting decade. Because of its scope, we imagine that it will be of value to historians working in a variety of disciplines, from literature and art to women's studies and popular culture. We have tried, however, to avoid the sorts of terms that would make it accessible only to academic readers. Instead, we hope that it can be dipped into profitably by anyone who is curious about a past and a society both remote and oddly familiar. Our greatest reward would be to hear that this volume had encouraged someone to pursue his or her own further explorations of the decade, uncovering what we may have overlooked. To borrow a phrase from Walter de la Mare, we hope most of all that "the confused catalogue that follows may be of service."

Neither our exhibition, The English Avant-Garde of the 1880s, held at the University of Virginia Library (2 February–31 March 1985), nor this catalogue would have been possible without the generosity of the following lenders: Cecil Y. Lang, William B. O'Neal, Franklin Gilliam Rare Books, and the University of Virginia Art Museum. All other materials, unless we have noted otherwise, are from the collections of the University of Virginia Library. Unless indicated otherwise, all books are first editions.

For their assistance, we are grateful to the staffs of the Rare Books and Manuscripts Departments; we also thank the following individuals: Julius Barclay, Curator of the Rare Books Department, and Edmund Berkeley, Jr., Curator of Manuscripts, as well as Mildred Abraham, Clinton Sisson, Judith Nelson, and Page Nelson-Saginor. We are grateful for the cooperation of Ruth Cross and of David Lawall, Director of the University of Virginia Art Museum. We would also like to acknowledge our photographer, Pauline Page of the University of Virginia Library. Special thanks are also due to David J. Holmes for his careful proofreading.

For their help, financial and otherwise, in making possible the concurrent symposium on the 1880s, we wish to thank Paul Barolsky and Malcolm Bell, Department of Art; Sharon Davie, Director of Women's Studies; Arthur Kirsch and the Department of English; William Harbaugh, Department of History and then chairman of the Richards and Page-Barbour Lectures Committees; Donald Loach, Department of Music; Dexter Whitehead and the Center for Advanced Studies; Shelah Scott and the Associates of the University of Virginia Library. The speakers who honored us with their presence at the symposium held on 2 February 1985 were Nina Auerbach, University of Pennsylvania; Jerome Hamilton Buckley, Harvard University; Donald D. Stone, Queens College, C.U.N.Y.; and Elliott Zuckerman, St. John's College, Annapolis.

Our thanks to: Pierre Coustillas and Michael Gissing, the author's grandson, for enabling us to publish Gissing letters; the literary estate of Thomas Hardy, for a letter previously printed in Richard Little Purdy and Michael Millgate's edition of *The Collected Letters of Thomas Hardy* (Oxford: Clarendon Press, 1978), 3:111; Oxford University Press for an extract from *The Letters of George Meredith*, ed. C. L. Cline (Oxford, 1970); Dan H. Laurence and the Society of Authors, as agents for the estate of George Bernard Shaw; Herbert M. Schueller for a letter printed in *The Letters of John Addington Symonds* (Detroit: Wayne State University Press, 1968), 2:712–13; and Sir Rupert Hart-Davis and Mr. Merlin Holland for permission to publish letters by Oscar Wilde. Material by Henry James has been reprinted by permission of Harvard University Press from *The Letters of Henry James*, ed. Leon Edel (Cambridge, 1980), 3:61, 128. Other manuscript material is published here with the permission of Edmund Berkeley, Jr., Curator of Manuscripts, and the Board of Visitors of the University of Virginia and with the permission of C. Waller Barrett.

Finally, we wish to acknowledge the enormous debt we owe to Jerome Hamilton Buckley, both for his kindness in allowing us to publish his Introduction and for his inspirational example as a scholar.

---

[1] Reid, in *The Eighteen-Eighties: Essays by Fellows of the Royal Society of Literature*, ed. Walter de la Mare (Cambridge: Cambridge University Press, 1930), 109; Eliot, ibid., 105.

[2] De la Mare, "Introduction," ibid., xxv.

ENGLAND IN THE 1880s

OLD GUARD AND AVANT-GARDE

INTRODUCTION

JEROME HAMILTON BUCKLEY

In June 1887 imperial Britain celebrated Queen Victoria's Golden Jubilee. Throngs of well-wishers greeted her arrival from Windsor at Paddington Station and vociferously cheered her progress to Buckingham Palace. Thirty thousand children were assembled to pay tribute in Hyde Park, and each for loyalty received in return a Jubilee mug and a currant bun. The queen generously pardoned a group of selected prisoners—all but one on the list, a felon guilty of cruelty to animals, for that, she said, was "one of the worst traits in human nature." All true Englishmen admired her pluck, and most shared her affection for dogs and horses. Her popularity was wide and deep, both at home and abroad. In 1880 she had received the Siamese Order of the White Elephant, an auspicious token perhaps, for at Jubilee time imperial fervor was reaching elephantine proportions.

Yet by 1887, in many real ways, the era that bears her name was virtually over. Many of the great Victorians left the scene during the eighties or shortly thereafter—Carlyle, George Eliot, Darwin, Disraeli, Arnold, Trollope, Browning, Newman, Tennyson. These had been among the principal creators of the mid-Victorian synthesis— by which I mean the interrelationship, sometimes easy, sometimes precarious, of art, ideas, science, religion, and social conscience in a plural culture. Henceforth no major scientist would be able to address a general public with Darwin's gift of literate exposition, and no major novelist would match George Eliot's understanding of scientific method and theory. One of Darwin's admirers complained wistfully, "I am getting to the point of thinking that the new men do not yet, at any rate, come up to the giants of olden days." Ruskin, who retreated to the shadows after 1885, declared the old harmony now broken and the whole world literally darkened by "the storm-cloud of the nineteenth century," until only "the ashes of the antipodes glare[d] through the night." (That cloud, we should note, was both fact and symbol, actually the long-lingering pollution from the 1883 eruption of Indonesian Krakatoa, an event far more spectacular than the recent explosions of Mount Saint Helens and Mauna Loa.)

The old ideal of synthesis did indeed seem to be yielding to a new demand for "specialism." According to the *New English Dictionary* (later known as the *OED*), the first fascicule of which appeared in 1884, "specialize" was a new verb in the eighties to describe a new attitude toward the arts, crafts, and sciences. To prosper henceforth one would have to "specialize," and to specialize meant almost inevitably to begin to lose sight of a general culture. Every decade, of course, is a time of transition, but the 1880s, more than most decades, seemed self-consciously to be moving in new directions. There were, as this catalogue abundantly testifies, many new figures offering notable new contributions, often of a specialized kind, to both science and literature. In the latter area (for I have no competence in the former), I should point to the literary debuts of Oscar Wilde, Bernard Shaw, George Gissing, George Moore, Rudyard Kipling, and William Butler Yeats, all of whom spoke from the outset with a new and quite un-Victorian accent.

If the conservatives of the eighties lamented the loss of the old giants, the avant-garde delighted in innovation and a saucy defiance of convention. Much of the novelty was visual or in some way theatrically conspicuous. James Tissot pictured the new young, well-to-do Englishmen in straw hats at carefree regattas, and John Singer Sargent brought his shockingly stylish portrait of the décolletée Madame X from Paris to London. Meanwhile, Oscar Wilde discovered America, found Niagara Falls "the earliest, if not the keenest, disappointment of American married life," and, when asked to lecture on aesthetics at a place called Griggsville, wired back, "Begin by changing the name of your town." After the Reform Bill of 1884 most men enjoyed the franchise, but not all used it, and from 1885 onward women, though still voteless, were cheerfully—when properly clad—admitted to the golf links. Gilbert and Sullivan provided the whole decade with innocent merriment, much of it directed at new modes and manners. *Princess Ida* glanced, not too sharply, at the growing sentiment called "womanism" (the term "feminism" seems not to have taken hold until the 1890s). And *Patience* hit at the props and jargon of the Aesthetic movement, the poppies and pallid lilies, the recent revivals of the Age of Anne and first French Empire, the late Pre-Raphaelite medievalism in its stained-glass attitudes, and the neo-Grecian drapery of the operetta's twenty lovesick maidens. At least among the affluent, a new era of elegance was dawning, and it seemed appropriate that the leadership of the beau monde had passed to the sophisticated, pleasure-loving Prince of Wales, who had officiated at the opening of the aesthetic Grosvenor Gallery, but whose interest in lovely shapes and figures was said to diminish rapidly as soon as they were transferred to canvas.

The general condition of England in the eighties, however, was far less salubrious than the well-being of the happy few might indicate. As the aging laureate, Tennyson chose to play Tiresias to his times, whether or not an acquisitive world would listen to his doom-ridden prophecies. In "Vastness" he pointed grimly to the juxtaposition of prosperous trade and economic misery, "Desolate offing, sailorless harbours, famishing populace, wharves forlorn." And in "Locksley Hall Sixty Years After," published just a year before the Jubilee, he deplored the failure of the mechanical Progress he had extolled in the first "Locksley Hall"; he was haunted now by visions of the hungry squalor of the new city ghettos, where "among the glooming alleys Progress halts on palsied feet." But at the same time—and in the same poem—he attacked the indecencies of "Zolaism," despite the fact that it was the English disciples of Zola, the new fictional realists, who were best equipped to dramatize the plight of the urban English poor. William Morris, we should remember, an artist far more radical than Tennyson, likewise rejected the mode of realism insofar as he saw in it a compromise with a rotten society, an attempt to make an artwork from repulsive materials. The avant-garde realists of the eighties, George Gissing and George Moore, accordingly found it difficult to interest any considerable reading public in the drab unloveliness of poverty and depression.

Unemployment, nonetheless, persisted throughout the decade, leading to riots and frequent demonstrations—the most ominous of all were the Bloody Sunday of 1887 at Trafalgar Square and the great Dock Strike of 1889. The very word "unemployed" as a noun to describe a whole class without work first gained currency in 1882, according to the *OED*. And there was, even in the year of Jubilee, at least one memorable literary expression of the problem—Gerard Manley Hopkins's powerful sonnet, "Tom's Garland," subtitled "upon the Unemployed," with its grim final couplet: "This, by Despair, bred Hangdog dull; by Rage / Manwolf, worse, and their packs infest the age." Glossing his cryptic idiom, Hopkins told Robert Bridges that he had been impatient "with the fools of Radical Levellers," until "presently I remember[ed] that this is all very well for those who are in, however low in, the Commonwealth and share in any way the Common weal; but that the curse of our times is that many do not share it, that they are outcasts from it and have neither security nor splendour, that they share care with the high and obscurity with the low, but wealth or comfort with neither."

William Morris independently had reached a similar conclusion, and in the eighties as an active socialist he wrote many earnest verses of protest, few of them rising above the level of incantatory doggerel. His most serious efforts, however, were turned to new political groups, the Social Democratic Federation and then the revolutionary Socialist League. Meanwhile, with more specialized objectives, the newly organized Fabian Society was articulating, with more practical reason than poetic fervor, Sidney Webb's program of reforming gradualism.

Other public issues, apart from unemployment, also troubled the decade. Economists argued with religious intensity the merits of bimetallism and the sanctity of the gold standard and pointed to the perils of an evil phenomenon to be called by a new Americanism, "inflation." The Lux Mundi controversy over a liberalized interpretation of Scripture rocked the Church of England. And the Irish Question, endlessly debated, exhausted the best—and worst—energies of both Commons and Lords. It was already quite evident even to the reactionary Lord Lytton that "our mismanagement of Ireland from first to last is unparalleled in the vivid and abundant annals of Human Ineptitude." Yet the most dramatic news of the eighties came from farther afield than Parnell's Dublin. In the Sudan, General Gordon, the archetypal Victorian hero, was besieged for ten months by the forces of a religious fanatic known as the Mahdi and was killed two days before the long-delayed arrival of a British rescue force— an event that profoundly agitated the Empire and precipitated the defeat of the aging prime minister Gladstone.

Our own decade clearly has not escaped similar anxieties. Yet a number of writers in the anxious eighties were eager to anticipate what they assumed would be the just and happy 1980s. One of them need not detain us long. In 1882 Anthony Trollope published one of the weakest of his many novels, *The Fixed Period*, the action of which transpires in Britannula in 1980. The prophetic content is hardly impressive; Trollope, whose best talents lay in other directions, imagined a steam tricycle that could accelerate to twenty-five miles an hour (a somewhat improbable answer to a future energy crisis). And the plot proves no less ineffectual, for Trollope, sixty-seven years old at the time of composition, withdrew his initial proposition that the citizens of Britannula would cheerfully accept self-sacrifice in Necropolis at the age of sixty-seven (an altruistic gesture quite unsatisfactory to aged politicians both then and now).

A more pertinent prophecy was the American Edward Bellamy's *Looking Backward,* a best-seller of 1888 on both sides of the Atlantic. Bellamy could have been influenced by the technological fantasies of Albert Robida, published with great success in Paris a few years earlier, predicting space travel and domestic television, women's liberation, and even, to Robida's unspeakable horror, women lawyers presiding over courts of justice. Bellamy's story is set in a new Boston, decontaminated but heavily industrialized, in the last quarter of the twentieth century, by which time society is well into its golden age and "for generations, rich and poor have been forgotten words." The change has brought regimentation, credit cards, total employment, machines of all kinds. The hero, Julian West, who has dreamed himself a hundred years ahead of the old Boston, is able to make himself useful as a kind of displaced academic, offering a history lecture course on the inequities of the 1880s.

Conceived as a conscious rejection of Bellamy's technocracy, William Morris's *News from Nowhere,* begun in 1889, conjures up a good, green, socialist England, demechanized and depolluted, which is to arise after a general strike and a Marxist revolution in the 1950s and 1960s. Nowhere has no crime, no greed, no money, and not much government—cooperative living apparently requires no compulsion. The Houses of Parliament are left standing, but only for the convenient storage of manure. There is little thought, or need for thinking, in this garden state, and certainly no sick introspection or pedantic scholarship, though eccentric antiquarians may still amuse themselves, if they wish, in the British Museum. Instead, there is a good deal of manual dexterity of a Scandinavian precision, and there is much evidence, everywhere in the village economy, of happily creative craftsmen singing while they work for the commonweal. *News from Nowhere* thus curiously combines Morris's two dominant impulses: his will to expose the social injustice of his age and his desire to lose himself in a world of lovely colors and beautiful, intricate patterns unsullied by contemporary bad taste.

Others found in the great world beyond little England a readier and more efficacious escape from the trials of domestic politics than utopian dreams of a serene late twentieth century could provide. Imperialism—the word itself in all its modern connotations was virtually an invention of the 1880s—diverted attention to the untapped resources of the ampler Britains abroad, and the "Jingoes," the most strident of the imperialists, did much to fan the flames of jingo fervor. The eighties were a decade of tireless travel, both within and beyond the far-flung Empire, both political (for imperial gain) and disinterested (for mere physical self-realization). The intrepid invalid Isabella Bird reported to eager readers her visit to the hairy Ainu of Hokkaido as the latest of her one-woman expeditions. H. M. Stanley continued to explore the dark heart of Africa, now partly for the Belgians in the Congo territory that was shortly to terrify the young Joseph Conrad. Laurence Oliphant attempted to establish a Jewish homeland in Palestine on the pattern of his own new colony at Haifa. C. M. Doughty enshrined his quasi-mystical view of Moslem culture in the mannered, archaic *Arabia Deserta*. And Richard Burton, long notorious for his exotic escapades everywhere from Mecca to Salt Lake City, issued his defiantly literal translation of the *Arabian Nights* in sixteen salacious volumes.

In such an ambiance fictions of adventure flourished as never before. The eighties introduced not only the unstable Dr. Jekyll and the dandified, enigmatic Sherlock Holmes against familiar British backgrounds but also new soldiers of fortune, adventurers on sea and land, in many more romantic settings. The remarkable success of Stevenson's *Treasure Island* in 1883 was followed not long after by the resounding hit of *King Solomon's Mines* by Rider Haggard and the even more sensational *She*. (Among Haggard's devoted admirers, incidentally, was an enthusiastic boy who came to him questioning a narrative detail: Winston Churchill, who some years later would chronicle his own hardly less incredible African exploits.) In 1888 Rudyard Kipling's *Plain Tales from the Hills* opened the doors to yet another country of romance, observed this time with a sharp eye for realities and delight in a vigorous vernacular. Indeed, all these books and authors widened the late Victorian perspective on empire, trade, manners, morals, and the more tangible items of taste and decor.

No longer could an art critic echo Ruskin's assured 1857 assertion that there was "no serious art beyond the confines of Europe." For now Japan was a new center of aesthetic attention. By 1885 Whistler, attacking Ruskin's moral aesthetic in the polished "Ten O'Clock" lecture, was ready, as Max Beerbohm remarked, to bring down "the table of Law . . . from the summit of Fujiyama." The rage for "all one sees / That's Japanese," signaled by *Patience*, became a leitmotiv of the decade. *The Mikado*, which opened in March 1885, tunefully exploited and so extended the vogue. Even William Ernest Henley, belligerent in other moods, yielded to the imagined gentle charm of a well-hairpinned Yum-Yum as he penned his "Ballade of a Toyokuni Colour-Print" with its sentimental refrain, "I loved you once in old Japan":

> *Clear shine the hills, the rice fields round*
> *Two cranes are circling; sleepy and slow*

A blue canal the lake's blue bound
Breaks at the bamboo bridge; and lo!
Touched with the sundown's spirit and glow,
I see you turn, with flirted fan,
Against the plum-tree's bloomy snow . . .
I loved you once in old Japan.

All of which was exceedingly dainty—and "daintiness," we learn, was one of Whistler's favorite criteria in calculating his "very aesthetic" Japanese arrangements.

The conspicuous new word of the eighties, however, was the noun "aesthete," and the Aesthetes were those who cultivated a sensibility exquisite enough to appreciate the elegance of old Japan and all other symbols of the dainty life. Among the Aesthetes there was often more pose than production, an egregious addiction to peacock feathers, sunflowers, and flirted fans. But even the serious artists who scorned the "Aesthetic" label felt a similar isolation from an unaesthetic Philistine public, at its deepest the loneliness of the sensitive man, as in Gissing's *Demos,* whose "heart is crushed by [the] uniformity of decent squalor" in north London. Some of these influenced the course of the Aesthetic movement and, beyond that, a lively avant-garde art of the future. Morris's natural geometries, his honeysuckle chintz, his intertwined acanthus wallpaper, his "Woodpecker" chintz, all anticipated the Art Nouveau, which in effect merely disentangled the curving forms from Morris's densely packed context. Burne-Jones's bemused maidens may seem, as Quentin Bell has suggested, all "beautiful and terribly anaemic" girls, who "will never blush and never put on weight and [whose] swains are not likely to help them do so." Nonetheless, in their static grace as parts of a pattern they were to interest the young Picasso, whose less languorous women also subserve a calculated design. Sargent's 1889 depiction of Ellen Terry as an ominous Lady Macbeth of some aesthetic order beyond good and evil seems to have prefigured the mood of the more aggressive feminism in the nineties. And Walter Sickert's picture of Katie Lawrence, the music-hall singer, was an early and bold adaptation of French impressionist techniques and a foreshadowing of the best later work of the New English Art Club. (It matters little that Katie, famous for her rendition of "Daisy, Daisy, give me your answer, do," took only a dim view of the reduction of herself to an aesthetic composition, a gauzy white apparition on a darkened stage.)

Though scarcely the "haggard and lank young man" evoked by *Patience,* Oscar Wilde was by common consent and his own contrivance the representative Aesthete of the eighties. As the tail-coated dandy caricatured by Ape (Carlo Pellegrini), Wilde confirmed the new elegance, even though he declared fashion a kind of ugliness so repulsive that it had to be changed every six months. At the same time he was eager to assert his unique difference. For his primary concern, before any large literary venture, was to devise a personal signature, and his effort to do so was thoroughly characteristic of his time.

Quite apart from the attitudes of the Aesthetes, the search for a more personal accent is apparent throughout the new literature. In his dedication to *Travels with a Donkey* (1879) Robert Louis Stevenson declared that "every book is, in an intimate sense, a circular letter to the friends of him who writes it. They alone take his meanings; they find private messages." Stevenson himself in his own "intimate" essays, especially *Virginibus Puerisque* (1881) and *Familiar Studies* (1882), cultivated a highly personal idiom—mannered, condensed, somewhat archaic. Had he needed one, the sanction for a self-regarding style might have been found in the theory and practice of Walter Pater, who now succeeded Matthew Arnold as the literary critic of most influence among the avant-garde. Pater saw the decline of the high Victorian synthesis, understood the sources of the new specialism, and sympathized with the retreat to personal values and the fear that one could be fully certain of nothing beyond the self and its flickering impressions.

In *Marius the Epicurean* (1885), Pater's oblique personal apologia, Marius indulges in the "modernism, . . . rare among the ancients," of keeping a private journal for introspection and self-communion. The subjective impulse, of course, had been strong among the earlier Victorians, but there it was largely controlled by a sense of responsibilities and realities beyond the self. Tennyson had chosen to express the intimacies of *In Memoriam* in a public as well as a private voice, "not always the author speaking of himself, but the voice of the human race speaking through him." And the great Victorian autobiographers—Newman, say, or John Stuart Mill—were concerned to relate their personal experience to their roles in society. But the new confessional writing was rather different in kind. Hopkins's "terrible sonnets" were freshly idiosyncratic in both style and substance, agonized cries from the depths of a unique sensibility. Henley's *In Hospital*, brutal in a new clinical mode, traced the course of a specific illness and one man's self-willed recovery. The new autobiography in prose was likewise more private than social, more often a self-creation than a balanced view of the actual subject. George Moore's *Confessions of a Young Man* (1888), for example, confessed as much to fantasy as to truth, and in the process evoked the sort of blasé expatriate that the young Moore aspired to be and was not. And John Addington Symonds's *Memoirs*, suppressed in manuscript for nearly a century and first published in 1984, probed with a curious blend of self-awareness and self-delusion the secret double life of a respectable monogamous man of letters who was also an obsessively promiscuous homosexual lover.

One autobiography, notorious in its time but now largely ignored, bears both the personal signature and the stamp of the eighties. *The Story of My Heart* by Richard Jefferies could scarcely have been written much earlier than 1883, or much later. It draws lightly on the facts of the author's life but heavily on the bravado that sustained it, the chronic invalid's praise of physical well-being, and on a defiant late Victorian paganism that revels in a universe "which is designless, and purposeless, and without idea." Jefferies's sensuous mysticism seems at times to foreshadow D. H. Lawrence's visionary creed: "I believe in the flesh and the body, which is worthy of worship—to see a perfect human body unveiled causes a sense of worship. The ascetics are the only persons who are impure. . . . Let me be fleshly perfect." Yet his cult of beauty, erotic as it is, is not far from the sexless affections of the Aesthetes. Attracted by the female charms depicted in the masterpieces of the National Gallery, Jefferies declared his aesthetic response: "I lived in looking; without beauty there is no life for me, the divine beauty of flesh is life itself to me." And though there was nothing of apparent elegance in the circumstances of his own sad experience, he could assert a wishful hedonism, heard in other tones throughout a decade seeking poise in the midst of change: "I cannot understand time. It is eternity now. I am in the midst of it. It is about me in the sunshine; I am in it, as the butterfly floats in the light-laden air. Nothing has to come; it is now. Now is eternity; now is the immortal life."

That, of course, was only a brave illusion; Jefferies's own span was pathetically short, and the eighties soon faded into the nineties. Only a work of art, a book, a picture, or an exhibition catalogue like this one can recover a snatch of lost time and stop it long enough for our edification and amusement.

THE OLD GUARD

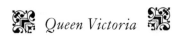
Queen Victoria

Throughout the spring and summer of 1887 all eyes were turned upon the many public ceremonies marking the occasion of Queen Victoria's Jubilee. At the height of these festivities, on 20 June 1887, the *Times* of London published some reflections upon her long reign and its impact upon the national life:

To-day the QUEEN completes the fiftieth year of a reign prosperous and glorious beyond any recorded in the annals of England. To few Sovereigns has it been granted to celebrate the Jubilee of their accession, and among these few we know of no Queen or Empress. In the early morning on the 20th of June, 1837, the ARCHBISHOP of CANTERBURY and the LORD CHAMBERLAIN hastened to Kensington Palace to rouse the young PRINCESS VICTORIA from her sleep and to announce to her that by her uncle's death she had succeeded to the Throne. From that moment onwards the QUEEN has been deeply impressed with the responsibilities of power, and has held her sovereignty to be a sacred trust for the benefit of the peoples under her rule. No constitutional Monarch has shown a more consistent respect for popular liberties or a clearer conception of royal duties. The QUEEN has this week the reward she must prize beyond all else, the spontaneous expression of national enthusiasm. The spectacle, which will culminate in the splendour of to-morrow's Thanksgiving Service in Westminster Abbey, in the Royal Procession through the streets, and in the illuminations of the evening, may well fix the attention, not only of all sorts and conditions of Englishmen, Scotchmen, and Irishmen, but of exalted and eminent personages from all civilized States. The Sovereigns of Europe will be fully represented in the historic scene, and seldom, perhaps, have so many princely visitors assembled to take part in such a ceremony. . . . But the most impressive element in the scene will be the demeanour of the people. Britons, in spite of a confirmed habit of grumbling, look upon their ancient institutions with steadfast affection and reverence, and their attachment to the monarchy has been blended with respect for the character of the QUEEN. Nothing in the rich and various history of the past fifty years is more worthy of record than the purification and refinement of social life and manners to which the influence of the Court has most powerfully contributed. Those who are familiar with the current literature of the early part of the century will most readily acknowledge how vast a change has taken place in the tone in which royalty and royal persons are spoken of. That change is mainly due to the conduct of the QUEEN, in public and in private, since her accession, and to the wisdom of the counsels by which she was long guided. It must ever be remembered that for this and other faithful services the nation owes a deep debt of gratitude to the memory of the PRINCE CONSORT.

As this newspaper account of the Jubilee suggests, Queen Victoria was as important a social icon in her lifetime as she was a monarch. By the 1880s her solemn, plump, and matronly countenance had become the symbol of the ideals of morality and dignity that guided middle-class English life. She stood for reticence and restraint in all matters, whether political, social, or artistic. To her eldest daughter she wrote in 1858, "Above all, dear, do remember never to lose the modesty of a young girl towards others . . . though you are married don't become a matron at once to whom everything can be said, and who minds saying nothing herself—I remained particular to a degree (indeed feel so now) and often feel shocked at the confidences of other married ladies." Almost single-handedly, she redefined for her age what it meant to be a lady, and she remained, for those of her contemporaries who lived to the end of the century, the exemplar of femininity.

Although the ruler of the most powerful and most rapidly expanding empire in the world, she presented herself first and above all else as the devoted wife of her consort, Prince Albert, and, after his death in 1861, as his eternally grieving widow. Her appearance in the 1880s was that of a relict in mourning—the flesh-and-blood equivalent of the black-bordered writing paper, jet beads, and watch chains made of hair clipped from the dead that were favored by her contemporaries in their bereavements. By the generation that was passing she was greatly loved, as much in the solitude and retirement of her old age as she had been in the girlish vitality of her youth, as a lasting image of revered womanhood. But to the generation coming to its intellectual and artistic maturity in the 1880s, her impassivity, stolidity, and growing decrepitude were also symbolic, ominously so. For the Aesthetes, for the social and intellectual rebels, and for women seeking the right to vote or to enter the professions, the figure of Queen Victoria would represent the mighty obstacles and opposition to be faced.

1. Sir George Hayter (1792–1871). *Study of Queen Victoria Opening Parliament*. Pencil drawing, 1838. (Lent by William B. O'Neal)
   This sketch of the youthful queen is a preliminary study for an oil painting of the subject now in the National Portrait Gallery, London. George Hayter's success in portraying Victoria led to his devoting almost all his talent to the depiction of royal personages.

2. Victoria, queen of England (1819–1901). Manuscript signed, commission for an army officer dated 21 June 1858.

3. John Baptiste Guth (?–1921). *A CIMIEZ. Promenade matinale: Her Majesty the Queen-Empress*. Color lithograph, caricature of Queen Victoria published in *Vanity Fair*, 17 June 1897. (Lent by Cecil Y. Lang)

The Poet Laureate

4. Alfred, Lord Tennyson (1809–1892). Autograph manuscript of "The Charge of the Light Brigade."
   A fair copy of Alfred, Lord Tennyson's most famous poem, which was written in 1854, this manuscript is signed by the author and dated 10 April 1864. It is tempting to believe that it was given by the poet to the Italian revolutionary hero Giuseppe Garibaldi, who was visiting the Tennysons on the Isle of Wight at the time.

5. Charles Lucy (1814–1873). *Portrait of Alfred Tennyson*. Oil on board, ca. 1865–70. (Lent anonymously)
   This painting of Tennyson is possibly a finished study for one of the portraits of eminent men commissioned from Charles Lucy by Sir Joshua Walmsley and now in the Victoria and Albert Museum, London.

6. Ape [Carlo Pellegrini (1839–1889)]. *The Poet Laureate: Alfred Tennyson*. Color lithograph, published in *Vanity Fair*, 22 July 1871. (Lent by Cecil Y. Lang)

7. Alfred, Lord Tennyson. *Hands All Round: A National Song.* London, [1882].

First published in the *Examiner* in 1852, this patriotic poem was considerably revised—indeed, virtually rewritten—for this edition issued in honor of Queen Victoria's birthday in 1882. The musical setting, described on the title page as having been "arranged and edited" by C. Villiers Stanford (1852–1924), actually was composed by Tennyson's wife, Emily (1813–1896). Sir Charles Tennyson's biography of his grandfather records the protests against the poem received by Tennyson from members of the Temperance movement, who objected to the line "To the great cause of Freedom drink, my friends." The port-imbibing poet laureate had to reply that the word "drink" referred to the "common cup . . . of unity" and not to alcohol.

8. Alfred, Lord Tennyson. *The Cup and The Falcon.* 1st published ed. London, 1884.

From the mid-1870s on, Tennyson devoted much of his energy to the writing of poetic dramas on historical subjects. When produced on the stage, his early plays *Queen Mary* (1876) and *The Falcon* (1879) were modest successes respectfully received by the critics. *The Cup,* based on a story from Plutarch, was greeted with almost universal acclaim when it opened in July 1881 with Ellen Terry and Henry Irving in the cast. Encouraged by this hit, Tennyson continued to write for the theater for the rest of the decade; but the only one of his later plays to be produced in London (and the only one to deal with contemporary life), *The Promise of May,* proved a complete failure.

This volume, which couples *The Cup* with the earlier *The Falcon,* was the first regularly published edition; Tennyson had already printed the two plays privately as "proofs," as was his habit with new works. The author inscribed this copy to his friend Frederick Locker (1821–1895), remembered now as a book collector and as the writer of the much-reprinted *London Lyrics* (1857). As in other presentation copies of this book, Tennyson wrote additional lines on page [86], to be inserted at a point he marked on page 80.

9. Alfred, Lord Tennyson. *Locksley Hall, Sixty Years After, Etc.* London, 1886.

The pessimism of this volume's title poem shocked the public on the eve of Queen Victoria's Jubilee year. Particularly upsetting was Tennyson's "repudiation" of the "progress" that had been made during the narrator's, and Tennyson's own, eighty-year life. W. E. Gladstone criticized the poem in a long review for the *Nineteenth Century*, concluding that "Justice does not require, nay rather she forbids, that the Jubilee of the Queen be marred by tragic notes." After such a protest it was not surprising that Tennyson responded with *Carmen Saeculare*, a much less controversial and more official Jubilee ode.

This copy of *Locksley Hall* is signed by Tennyson and has the ownership inscription of his nephew Walter Ker, a legal scholar and minor poet.

10. Alfred, Lord Tennyson. *Carmen Saeculare*. London, 1887. See fig. 1.

This is the first separate edition of Tennyson's Jubilee ode, which had previously appeared in the April 1887 issue of *Macmillan's Magazine*. Tennyson presented this copy to William Gordon McCabe (1841–1920), a former University of Virginia student and Confederate veteran who had become a schoolmaster and man of letters in Petersburg and Richmond. In the 1880s McCabe made several trips to England, where through Anne Thackeray Ritchie (novelist and daughter of W. M. Thackeray) he came to know many literary figures. McCabe's papers, which include letters from Matthew Arnold and William Black, as well as from Tennyson, were a recent gift from his family to the University of Virginia Library.

11. Edward Lear (1812–1888). *Capo Sant'Angelo, Amalfi*. Ink and wash drawing, ca. 1880. (Lent by William B. O'Neal)

Remembered today primarily for his nonsense verses, Edward Lear was also a semiprofessional artist who published a number of illustrated travel books. In 1852 he began a series of illustrations to Tennyson's poems, connecting specific lines to particular landscapes he had seen. The whole group of drawings, some two hundred in all, was meant to be a parallel to J. M. W. Turner's *Liber Studiorum*, but Lear never found a suitable method of reproduction. Only twenty-two of the illustrations were printed in 1889 after his death, in a limited edition signed by Tennyson as a tribute to his friend's project. This drawing illustrates lines from "The Palace of Art":

> One show'd an iron coast and angry waves,
> You seem'd to hear them climb and fall
> And roar rock-thwarted under bellowing caves,
> Beneath the windy wall.

12. Edward Lear. *Mt. Kinchinjunga*. Ink and wash drawing, ca. 1880. (Lent by William B. O'Neal)

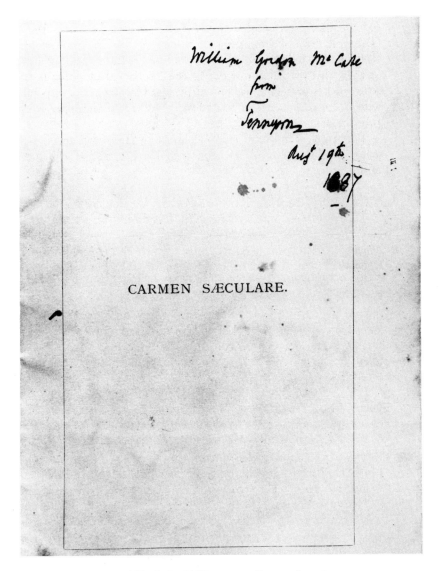

CARMEN SÆCULARE.

1. Alfred, Lord Tennyson, *Carmen Saeculare*
(London, 1887), presentation inscription to
W. Gordon McCabe (item 10)

Lear believed that this scene in Darjeeling, India, corresponded to lines from Tennyson's poem of 1853 addressed to him—"To E. L., on his Travels in Greece":

> Tomohrit, Athos, all things fair,
> With such a pencil, such a pen,
> You shadow forth to distant men,
> I read and felt that I was there.

This drawing was once in Tennyson's own collection.

The Literary Establishment

13. Coïdé [James Jacques Tissot (1836–1902)]. *"I say, the critic must keep out of the region of immediate practice": Matthew Arnold.* Color lithograph, published in *Vanity Fair*, 11 November 1871. (Lent by Cecil Y. Lang)

    The caption is a quotation from Matthew Arnold's "The Function of Criticism at the Present Time," published as the first essay in *Essays in Criticism* (1865).

14. Matthew Arnold (1822–1888). *The Matthew Arnold Birthday Book.* New York, 1883. See figs. 2 and 3.

    Matthew Arnold's popularity in the 1880s was demonstrated by the publication and sale of such ephemera as this—a compilation of wise sayings drawn from his works, interspersed with blank spaces for the use of the volume's owner.

15. Matthew Arnold. Autograph letter signed to Richard D'Oyly Carte (1844–1901), 9 October 1883. See fig. 4.

    Arnold's first American lecture tour lasted from October 1883 to March 1884. Here, shortly before his departure from England, he wrote to Richard D'Oyly Carte, the well-known impresario of the Savoy Theatre who had organized Arnold's tour.

16. Printed check endorsed by Matthew Arnold and made out to him by James Thomas Knowles (1831–1908), founding editor of the *Nineteenth Century*. Check dated 3 August 1882.

    Arnold received this payment for his article "Literature and Science," which appeared in the August 1882 issue of the *Nineteenth Century*. He revised the essay considerably for its later publication in *Discourses in America* (1885).

17. Matthew Arnold. *Discourses in America.* London, 1885.

    At Cambridge in 1882 Arnold issued, in the form of a lecture, his

2. *The Matthew Arnold Birthday Book* (New York, 1883), frontispiece (item 14)

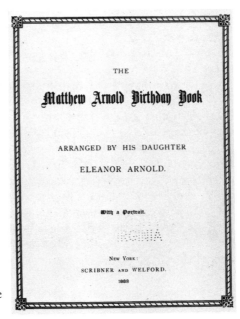

3. *The Matthew Arnold Birthday Book* (New York, 1883), title page (item 14)

4. Matthew Arnold, autograph letter to Richard
D'Oyly Carte (item 15)

reply to the attack made upon him by T. H. Huxley in "Science and Culture." This lecture, in a revised version, became part of the repertory of speeches used by Arnold on his tour of America in 1883–84. "Literature and Science," as it was titled for publication in this volume, offered a rebuttal to Huxley's claim that the principles of a classical education had become anachronistic and useless and expressed Arnold's own preference for art over science: "If then there is to be separation and option between humane letters on the one hand, and the natural sciences on the other, the great majority of mankind, all who have not exceptional and overpowering aptitudes for the study of nature, would do well, I cannot but think, to choose to be educated in humane letters rather than in the natural sciences. Letters will call out their being at more points, will make them live more."

18. Matthew Arnold. Autograph manuscript of *Special Report on Certain Points Connected with Elementary Education in Germany, Switzerland, and France,* May 1886.

This report, Arnold's last work as a school inspector, gives his observations made on visits to the Continent between November 1885 and March 1886. It was published later the same year in pamphlet form.

19. Matthew Arnold. Autograph letter signed to Arthur Howard Galton (1852–1921), 21 April 1887.

Arnold wrote to the *Hobby Horse*'s editor Arthur Howard Galton about submitting a poem to the magazine: "I do not like to undertake anything as to contributing. . . . But if I can make anything of a little Horatian Ode, in verse, which has lain by me for years, discarded because of an unsatisfactory stanza, you shall have it. . . . I shall be curious to see what Ruskin has done for you. His is indeed a popular influence; I will not say that a contribution from me could do you no service; but it is not to be compared, as a help with the great public, to one from J. Ruskin." The poem appeared with the title "Horation Echo" in the *Hobby Horse* in July 1887.

20. Matthew Arnold. *Essays in Criticism, Second Series.* London, 1888.

Of all Victorian critics, Matthew Arnold had been the most insistent upon the need for Englishmen to look beyond the confines of their own national culture. As he had said in "The Function of Criticism at the Present Time" (published in his first series of *Essays in Criticism,* 1865), "to those who have to deal with the mass—so much better disregarded—of current English literature, that they may at all events endeavour, in dealing with this, to try it, so far as they can, by the standard of the best that is known and thought in the world; one may say, that to get anywhere near this standard, every critic should try and possess one great literature, at least, besides his own; and the more unlike his own, the better." Arnold's own success in accomplishing this task is illustrated by "Count Leo Tolstoi," one of the essays that he chose for his second series of *Essays in Criticism*, which, however, did not appear until after his death in 1888.

21. Ape [Carlo Pellegrini]. *Modern Poetry: Robert Browning.* Color lithograph, published in *Vanity Fair*, 20 November 1875. (Lent by Cecil Y. Lang)

22. Robert Browning (1812–1889). *Bells and Pomegranates.* London, 1841–46.

After the commercial failure of his earlier books, Robert Browning decided to bring out his works in a less expensive series of pamphlets. The result was *Bells and Pomegranates*, made up of eight parts issued at irregular intervals between 1841 and 1846 and eventually bound up to form a single volume. Among the poems are "Pippa Passes," "The Pied Piper of Hamelin," "My Last Duchess," and "The Tomb at St. Praxed's" (as it was titled in this edition). The series also includes Browning's second play, *A Blot on the 'Scutcheon*, as its fifth part. First performed on 11 February 1843, the play had starred the actress Helen Faucit (1818–1898), who was married to Sir Theodore Martin, poet and biographer. Browning presented this copy to her with his "best thanks and respects."

23. *The Browning Society's Papers.* Part I. 2d rev. ed. London, 1884.

The increasing popularity of Browning's later books, together with what was believed to be their obscurity, led in 1881 to the formation of the Browning Society, one of a group of organizations started in the 1880s with the aim of applying scientific methods to literary study. The society, the first to be devoted to a living writer, was founded by Frederick J. Furnivall (1825–1910), who also began the Chaucer, New Shakespeare, and Shelley societies along similar lines. The membership included such figures as Arthur Symons, James Thomson, William Rossetti, and Karl Marx's daughter, Eleanor Marx-Aveling.

The society's collected papers were published in twelve parts; a second, revised edition of the first part appeared in 1884. Furnivall was a distinguished scholar who described himself as an "agnostic" and as a "radical and democrat"; it is, therefore, not surprising that the publication he edited contains, along with a detailed bibliography of Browning's work, a reprint of the poet's essay on Shelley, originally a preface to a volume of spurious Shelley letters issued in 1852.

24. Robert Browning. *Asolando: Fancies and Facts*. London, 1890.

Preceded in Browning's oeuvre of the 1880s by long dramatic monologues and by translations from Euripides and Aristophanes, *Asolando* offered instead a series of unconnected shorter lyric poems. This was Browning's last book, published coincidentally on the day of his death, 12 December 1889. It was common practice for Victorian books published late in the year to be postdated.

25. William Wilkie Collins (1824–1889). *Heart and Science: A Story of the Present Time*. 3 vols. London, 1883.

Wilkie Collins, whose major successes had come in 1859–60 (*The Woman in White*) and 1868 (*The Moonstone*) was representative of an older generation of Victorian writers in his close authorial relationship with his middle-class audience and in his regard for that public's tastes. He began his antivivisectionist novel *Heart and Science* with a preface addressed to "Readers in General" in which he made plain his willingness to entertain the audience in return for its love:

> You are the children of Old Mother England, on both sides of the Atlantic; you form the majority of buyers and borrowers of novels; and you judge of works of fiction by certain inbred preferences, which but slightly influence the other great public of readers on the continent of Europe.
>
> The two qualities in fiction which hold the highest rank in your estimation are: Character and Humour. . . .
>
> Still persisting in telling you a story—still refusing to get up in the pulpit and preach, or to invade the platform and lecture, or to take you by the buttonhole in confidence and make fun of my Art—it has been my chief effort to draw the characters with a vigour and breadth of treatment, derived from the nearest and truest view that I could get of the one model, Nature. Whether I shall at once succeed in adding to the circle of your friends in the world of fiction—or whether you will hurry through the narrative, and only discover on a later reading that it is the characters which have interested you in the story— remains to be seen. Either way, your sympathy will find me grateful; for, either way, my motive has been to please you.

26. [Benjamin Disraeli, first earl of Beaconsfield (1804–1881)]. *Endymion. By the Author of Lothair*. 3 vols. London, 1880.

In a letter of 21 February 1881 Matthew Arnold reported:

On Friday night I had a long talk with Lord Beaconsfield at Lady Airlie's. He was in a good humour, and had evidently resolved to be civil. He got up, took me to a settee at the end of the room, and said, pointing to it—The poet's sofa! I told him of my having mentioned to Gladstone some of the epigrammatic things in *Endymion*, and he said—'But I don't want to talk about my things, I want to talk about *you*.' He went on to say that he read me with delight, that I was doing very great good, and ended by declaring that I was the only living Englishman who had become a classic in his own lifetime.

In his desire to be "civil" to Arnold, Benjamin Disraeli was perhaps guilty of excessive modesty, for at the end of his life he himself was not merely a "classic" but a legend in the fields of literature, oratory, and especially politics. Descendant of a Sephardic Jewish family which had only established itself in England in the 1740s, he nevertheless rose through the ranks of Parliament to become prime minister twice (February to December 1868 and 1874–80), to receive a title, and to be one of the privileged few to whom Queen Victoria turned for advice and friendship. All this he accomplished while producing a sizable body of multivolume novels which, with their exhaustive attention to the political problems of the day, embodied the heavy didacticism soon to be rejected by the rising authors of the 1880s.

27. Spy [Sir Leslie Ward (1851–1922)]. *A Novelist: Anthony Trollope.* Color lithograph published in *Vanity Fair*, 5 April 1873. (Lent by Cecil Y. Lang)

Anthony Trollope was typical of his mid-Victorian literary contemporaries in his insistence upon the moral function of art. As he wrote in "Novel-Reading: The Works of Charles Dickens; The Works of W. Makepeace Thackeray," an essay published in January 1879 in the *Nineteenth Century*:

> To the novelist, thinking of all this, it must surely become a matter of deep conscience how he shall handle those characters by whose words and doings he hopes to interest his readers. . . . The writer of stories must please, or he will be nothing. And he must teach, whether he wish to teach or not. How shall he teach lessons of virtue, and at the same time make himself a delight to his readers? Sermons in themselves are not thought to be agreeable; nor are disquisitions on moral philosophy supposed to be pleasant reading for our idle hours. But the novelist, if he have a conscience, must preach his sermons with the same purpose as the clergyman, and must have his own system of ethics. If he can do this efficiently, if he can make virtue

alluring and vice ugly, while he charms his reader instead of wearying him, then we think that he should not be spoken of generally as being among those workers of iniquity who do evil in their generation.

Although, even in his works of the 1880s, Trollope would still hold to the principle of using fiction to instruct and improve the reader, the decade's new generation of novelists, influenced by the example of the French Naturalists, would come to reject his analogy between artists and clergymen. They would refuse not only to teach the middle-class public but also to entertain or "please" it in Trollope's fashion.

28. Anthony Trollope (1815–1882). Autograph letter signed to George Eliot [Mary Ann Evans (1819–1880)], 18 October 1863.

   In this letter to his fellow realist, Anthony Trollope outlined the aesthetic that would guide him throughout his career: "You know that my novels are not sensational. In Rachel Ray [a novel published in 1863] I have attempted to confine myself absolutely to the commonest details of commonplace life among the most ordinary people, allowing myself no incident that would be even remarkable in every day life. I have shorn my fiction of all romance."

29. Anthony Trollope. *The Fixed Period: A Novel.* 2 vols. Edinburgh, 1882.

   Near the end of his career, Trollope wrote this uncharacteristically pessimistic fantasy, first published in *Blackwood's Magazine*, October 1881–March 1882. A "dystopian" story of life in the future, it is set in the imaginary English colony of "Britannula" where the government has decided upon a policy of genocide for the old. The "fixed period" of the title refers to the number of years that each citizen is allowed to live before he must be put to death.

   This was Trollope's own copy of one of the rarest of his first editions, with his bookplate in the first volume. It was for many years in the library of Michael Sadleir (1888–1957), Trollope's biographer and bibliographer.

30. Anthony Trollope. *An Autobiography.* 2 vols. Edinburgh, 1883.

   Trollope's account of his own life proved unexpectedly controversial, for it contained a record of the sales of his many novels and of the profits he had earned from them. The matter-of-factness with which he discussed not only commercial aspects of his profession but also his extremely disciplined and regular methods of working to schedule alienated many middle-class readers who preferred to think of artists as divinely inspired beings, above such material cares.

This copy is inscribed "With the compliments of the publisher, Mr. Blackwood."

 *Science and Philosophy*

31. Charles Darwin (1809–1882). *The Origin of Species by Means of Natural Selection, or the Preservation of Favoured Races in the Struggle for Life*. 6th ed. London, 1872.

Perhaps the most crucial event determining the course of late Victorian intellectual history came almost at mid-century—the publication in 1859 of Charles Darwin's scientific treatise on the adaptation and development through time of all life-forms in nature. In shaping the spirit of the coming age, no concept in this groundbreaking work was more influential than that of natural selection through competition. As Darwin explained in the third chapter: "A struggle for existence inevitably follows from the high rate at which all organic beings tend to increase. . . . Hence, as more individuals are produced than can possibly survive, there must in every case be a struggle for existence, either one individual with another of the same species, or with the individuals of distinct species, or with the physical conditions of life."

The social scientists, known as Social Darwinists, who followed in his wake tended to apply this biological notion prescriptively to human civilization. Led by Herbert Spencer, these social theorists argued that the future of the race depended upon the "survival of the fittest"—of the strongest individuals, who could best demonstrate their "fitness" by overcoming their weaker opponents in a highly competitive economic and social system. The resulting callousness of the middle classes, who saw themselves as the "fittest," toward the lower classes caused young intellectuals of the 1880s, such as George Gissing, to rail against this destructive principle of the "battle of life" and also helped to turn William Morris from an artist into a socialist.

This copy of the sixth edition is inscribed by the author to William Sweetland Dallas (1824–1890), a naturalist who supported Darwin's views in a series of books and who translated from German Fritz Müller's *Facts and Arguments for Darwin* (1869).

32. Julia Margaret Cameron (1815–1879). Photograph of Charles Darwin. Silver print, 1868. See fig. 5.

This is one of only a few copies inscribed by Darwin, who wrote, "I like this photograph very much better than any other which has

5. Julia Margaret Cameron, photograph of
Charles Darwin (item 32)

been taken of me." Julia Cameron, known both for her images of poets such as Tennyson and for her personal eccentricities, was surprised when Darwin offered to pay for his portrait.

33. Charles Darwin. Autograph letter signed to an unidentified recipient, 2 November [after 1862].

In defense of his controversial views on evolution, Darwin wrote:

No one could dissent from my views on the modification of species with more courtesy than you do. But from the tenor of your mind I feel an entire & comfortable conviction (& which cannot possibly be disturbed) that if your studies led you to attend much to general questions in Natural History, you would come to the same conclusions that I have done.

Have you ever read Huxley's little book of Six Lectures? I would gladly send you a copy if you think you would read it.

Considering what Geology teaches us, the argument for the supposed immutability of specific Types seems to me much the same as if, in a nation which had no old writings, some wise old savage was to say that his language had never changed; but my metaphor is too long to fill up.

34. Caricatures of Charles Darwin, ca. 1870–80.

In the conclusion of *The Origin of Species*, Darwin said, "I believe that animals have descended from at most only four or five progenitors, and plants from an equal or lesser number. Analogy would lead me one step further, namely, to the belief that all animals and plants have descended from some one prototype." Contemporary newspaper cartoonists fastened gleefully on this notion of "descent" (which Darwin explored more fully in *The Descent of Man*, 1871) in lampooning the great evolutionist, whom they often depicted with simian jaw and curling tail, as still half-ape himself.

35. Ticket of admittance and program for Darwin's funeral, 26 April 1882.

36. Photograph of Emma Wedgwood (1808–1896), widow of Charles Darwin. Collotype print, ca. 1890.

In a decade of change, the rules of social behavior, particularly for women, nevertheless remained quite strict. The author of the popular handbook *Manners and Rules of Good Society* (1888) advised:

The regulation period for a widow's mourning is two years. Of this period crape should be worn for one year and nine months—for the first twelve months the dress should be entirely covered with crape, and for the remaining three months trimmed with crape; during the last three months black without crape should be worn. After two years, half-mourning is prescribed.

The widow's cap should be worn for a year and a day. Lawn cuffs and collars should be worn during the crape period.

Widowers should wear mourning for the same period as widows, but they usually enter society much sooner. A widow is not expected to enter into society under twelve months, and during that time she should neither accept invitations nor issue them.

For the older generation of women, however, Queen Victoria, dressed in her unvarying weeds, set the standard for proper deportment. The effect of the queen's example upon her contemporaries may be seen in this photograph of Mrs. Charles Darwin, who more than eight years after the death of her husband still wore the badges of her widowhood.

37. Thomas Henry Huxley (1825–1895). [*Charles Darwin.*] London, 1882.

This pamphlet, probably issued for circulation among Darwin's friends, reprinted the obituary notice that had appeared originally in the *Proceedings of the Royal Society.*

38. Caricature of Charles Darwin and T. H. Huxley. Watercolor, ca. 1860–70.

The unattributed drawing shows the father of the theory of the adaptation of species with his chief public champion.

39. Photograph of Thomas Henry Huxley, scientist, educational theorist, and philosopher. Albumen print, ca. 1870.

40. Thomas Henry Huxley. *Critiques and Addresses*. London, 1873.

Among the essays collected in this volume was "Mr. Darwin's Critics," a survey of contemporary reaction to the theory of evolution, in which T. H. Huxley took note of the gradual shift in opinion that was occurring. As he recorded with obvious pleasure, "The mixture of ignorance and insolence which, at first, characterised a large proportion of the attacks with which he was assailed, is no longer the sad distinction of anti-Darwinian criticism."

This is an inscribed presentation copy from Huxley to Herbert Spencer.

41. Thomas Henry Huxley. *Science and Culture and Other Essays*. London, 1881.

In 1880 Matthew Arnold began his essay called "The Study of Poetry" (first published as the introduction to *The English Poets*, edited by T. H. Ward, and later reprinted in *Essays in Criticism, Second Series*, 1888) by saying:

> The future of poetry is immense, because in poetry, where it is worthy of its high destinies, our race, as time goes on, will find an ever surer and surer stay. There is not a creed which is not shaken, not an accredited dogma which is not shown to be questionable, not a received tradition which does not threaten to dissolve. Our religion has materialised itself in the fact, and now the fact is failing it. But for poetry the idea is everything; the rest is a world of illusion, of divine illusion. Poetry attaches its emotion to the idea; the idea *is* the fact. The strongest part of our religion to-day is its unconscious poetry.

Since the 1830s, when new geological evidence about the Creation had begun to overturn the "supposed fact," science had been viewed by the Victorian public as the destroyer of religion and of faith. The major blows against "accredited dogma," however, were not struck until 1859, with the publication of Darwin's *The Origin of Species*, and 1860, when T. H. Huxley, the most articulate and pugnacious of the evolutionists, issued his notorious reply to the bishop of Oxford. As the prop of Christianity failed them, more and more intellectuals fled, as Arnold did, to art as a "surer stay." For Arnold, the survival of civilization depended upon the spread of literary culture—especially, upon increased familiarity with those works of the past usually studied as part of a classical education.

But in the 1880s scientists—not content, it seemed, with their victory over theology—turned their weapons against humane letters, the new refuge. On 1 October 1880, at the opening ceremonies for Sir Josiah Mason's Science College in Birmingham, Huxley delivered the address later published in this volume as "Science and Culture." In it, Huxley offered a direct challenge to Arnold and to all "Humanists," as he called them, announcing:

> For I hold very strongly by two convictions: The first is, that neither the discipline nor the subject-matter of classical education is of such direct value to the student of physical science as to justify the expenditure of valuable time upon either; and the second is, that for the purpose of attaining real culture, an exclusively scientific education is at least as effectual as an exclusively literary education.

42. Contemporary photograph of Herbert Spencer (1820–1903), philosopher, sociologist, and evolutionist. Albumen print, ca. 1870.

Herbert Spencer, who would be famous in the 1880s for his methods of applying scientific principles to social theory, was an early advocate of the "development hypothesis," as it was called—a preliminary step toward Darwin's theory of "descent." Spencer wrote in the 20 March 1852 issue of the *Leader,* foreshadowing Arnold's description of how "the fact" would "fail" religion:

> Which, then, is the most rational hypothesis; that of special creations which has neither a fact to support it nor is even definitely conceivable; or that of modification, which is not only definitely conceivable, but is countenanced by the habitudes of every existing organism? . . .
>
> We have, indeed, in the part taken by many scientific men in this controversy of 'Law *versus* Miracle,' a good illustration of the tenacious vitality of superstitions. Ask one of our leading geologists or physiologists whether he believes in the Mosaic account of the creation, and he will take the question as next to an insult. Either he rejects the narrative entirely, or understands it in some vague non-natural sense. Yet . . . whence has he got this notion of 'special creations,' which he thinks so reasonable, and fights for so vigorously? Evidently he can trace it back to no other source than this myth which he repudiates. He has not a single fact in nature to quote in proof of it; nor is he prepared with any chain of abstract reasoning by which it may be established. Catechise him, and he will be forced to confess that the notion was put into his mind in childhood as part of a story which he now thinks absurd.

43. Herbert Spencer. Autograph letter signed to John Chapman (1821–1894), 11 November 1859.

Spencer wrote to John Chapman, editor of the *Westminster Review:*
> The two articles which I want to write on this development question will be the one destructive and the other constructive—the one a trenchant, and I think a crushing criticism of the arguments of opponents, and the other the presentation in a coherent shape of the enormous amount of valid evidence (chiefly indirect) which has been hitherto but little appealed to. . . . And then I propose showing how completely the doctrine of development as consequent on adaptations harmonizes with all advanced views on Politics, Theology, Education, Psychology, etc., etc.

44. Herbert Spencer. *First Principles.* 4th ed. London, 1880.

This was the first volume of Spencer's comprehensive theoretical work, *A System of Synthetic Philosophy.* Other volumes included *Principles of Biology* (1864–67), *Principles of Psychology* (rev. ed., 1870–72), and *Principles of Sociology* (1876–96). This is the author's own copy, with his ink ownership stamp on the title page.

THE AESTHETES

The Pre-Raphaelites and Their Associates

45. Adriano Cecioni (1838–1886). *The Realization of the Ideal: John Ruskin.* Color lithograph published in *Vanity Fair,* 17 February 1872. (Lent by Cecil Y. Lang)
    Nowadays, this wicked portrait of the author of *The Stones of Venice* is virtually the only work of the Italian caricaturist that is still remembered.

46. John Ruskin (1819–1900). *Architectural Study.* Watercolor, ca. 1842. (Lent by William B. O'Neal)
    As well as a critic of art and society, John Ruskin was a talented watercolorist who had studied with Copley Fielding and J. D. Harding. For all his admiration of Turner, he did not emulate his hero's techniques in his own works; instead, as in his writings on painting and architecture, he concentrated on observing closely and reproducing exactly details of nature and of buildings. If, as is believed, this drawing is of Bruges, then it was probably executed in 1842 on Ruskin's second trip to the city.

47. John Ruskin. *Sesame and Lilies: Two Lectures Delivered in Manchester in 1864.* London, 1865.
    This extremely popular volume is composed of two lectures, "Of Kings' Treasuries" and "Of Queens' Gardens." The latter of these, Ruskin's attempt to prescribe the appropriate cultural and moral education for young ladies, offers perhaps the most articulate and comprehensive statement of the mid-Victorian period about the role of women:

> The man's power is active, progressive, defensive. . . . But the
> woman's power is for rule, not for battle—and her intellect is not for

invention or creation, but for sweet ordering, arrangement, and decision. . . . The man, in his rough work in open world, must encounter all peril and trial. . . . But he guards the woman from all this; within his house, as ruled by her, unless she herself has sought it, need enter no danger, no temptation, no cause of error or offence. This is the true nature of home—it is the place of Peace. . . .

And wherever a true wife comes, this home is always round her. . . . She must be enduringly, incorruptibly good; instinctively, infallibly wise—wise, not for self-development, but for self-renunciation: wise, not that she may set herself above her husband, but that she may never fall from his side.

Many middle-class men and women of the later Victorian age still held to Ruskin's ideal of separate spheres of duty and activities for the sexes. But the New Woman of the 1880s—the rebellious female in pursuit of suffrage, a university education, professional qualifications, and the freedom to enter the "open world"—came to view the argument contained in "Of Queens' Gardens" and similar Ruskinian pronouncements as false and pernicious.

This copy is inscribed by the author to Sybil Noyes, June 1865.

48. Elliott and Fry. Photograph of John Ruskin. Collotype print, London, 1882. (Lent anonymously)

49. John Ruskin. *Praeterita: Outlines of Scenes and Thoughts Perhaps Worthy of Memory in My Past Life.* Orpington, Kent, 1885–89.

Later published in three bound volumes, Ruskin's autobiography was issued first in twenty-eight parts, from July 1885 to July 1889. The first chapter, "The Springs of Wandel," contains the remarkable story of Ruskin's childhood, which was blighted by the religious fanaticism of a mother who had "devoted him to God" from his birth and intended him to be a clergyman. Although he was forbidden both toys and the company of other children, Ruskin grew to believe that this early deprivation actually had been beneficial, forcing him to develop his powers of observation and preparing him to become an artist and aesthetic critic: "when I was five or six years old . . . [I] could pass my days contentedly in tracing the squares and comparing the colours of my carpet—examining the knots in the wood of the floor, or counting the bricks in the opposite houses . . . what patterns I could find in bed-covers, dresses, or wall-papers to be examined, were my chief resources."

50. Dante Gabriel Rossetti (1828–1882). *Mrs. William Morris.* Pencil drawing, 1870. (Lent anonymously)

By the end of the 1860s Dante Gabriel Rossetti's love for his friend

William Morris's wife, Jane, had established her as the principal inspiration for both his painting and his poetry. Her attitude and dress in such stylized depictions as *Pandora* (1871), *Proserpine* (1877), and *Astarte Syriaca* (1877) had a profound influence upon the images of languorous women so common in painting of the 1880s.

51. W. and D. Downey. Photograph of Dante Gabriel Rossetti. Albumen print, London, ca. 1862–68. (Lent anonymously)

52. Dante Gabriel Rossetti. *Poems*. London, 1870.
   This book, by the circumstances of its publication, by its contents, and by its design, secured Rossetti's reputation. When his wife, Elizabeth Siddal Rossetti, died in February 1862, Rossetti placed the original manuscripts of his poems in her coffin. In 1869 these were exhumed secretly from her grave and published in this volume in 1870 with other, more recent, work. The book opens with "The Blessed Damozel," Rossetti's most famous poem, which had first appeared in the Pre-Raphaelite magazine, the *Germ*, in 1850; among the other contents are the sonnet sequence called "The House of Life" and a group of poems about paintings that show Rossetti's abiding interest in unifying the sister arts. One of these poems is "The Wine of Circe," a sonnet describing a large watercolor painted in 1863–69 by Rossetti's disciple Sir Edward Burne-Jones.
   Poems (1870) was perhaps most remarkable for being one of the first books to be designed throughout by an author. Over a period of nine months, Rossetti supervised the printing of the proofs while painstakingly designing the covers and endpapers. The result had a great influence upon writers and designers of the 1880s. Oscar Wilde's *Poems* (1881) and several of Walter Pater's books clearly were modeled upon Rossetti's unique volume.

53. Dante Gabriel Rossetti. Autograph letter signed to Theodore Watts-Dunton (1832–1914), Sunday [1878?].
   Written to Rossetti's solicitor, Theodore Watts-Dunton, who later immortalized Rossetti in his roman à clef titled *Aylwin* (1898), this letter seems to refer to a dinner held by James McNeill Whistler at his new house (designed by E. W. Godwin in 1877) to celebrate the founding of *Piccadilly*, a short-lived magazine edited by Watts-Dunton and Whistler.

54. Dante Gabriel Rossetti. *Ballads and Sonnets*. Large-paper issue. London, 1881.

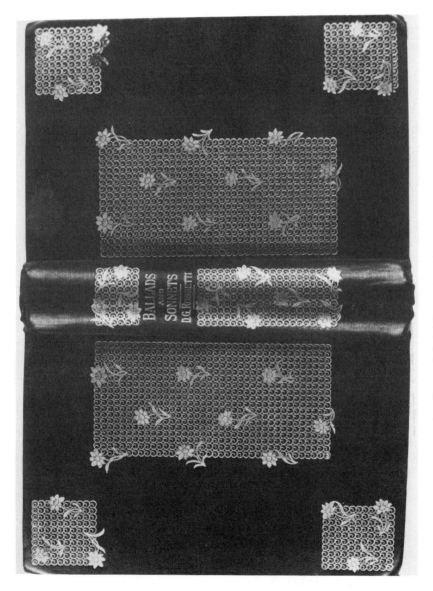

6.   Dante Gabriel Rossetti, *Ballads and Sonnets* (London, 1881), cover design (item 55)

In 1880 Rossetti decided to republish his literary works in two volumes, *Poems* and *Ballads and Sonnets*. Both were issued in 1881 and contained not only the entire contents of his 1870 book but many new poems, including an augmented version of "The House of Life" and a series of sonnets dealing with his own pictures. Although this copy bears the legend "Twenty-five copies printed on large paper for Subscribers only," probably as many as thirty were produced by the publisher for sale at a premium. All the known copies inscribed by Rossetti to his friends are of the ordinary trade edition.

55. Dante Gabriel Rossetti. *Ballads and Sonnets*. Regular issue. London, 1881. See fig. 6.

For the small-paper copies of this book, Rossetti insisted that his publishers use the binding and decorative endpapers that he had designed for his *Poems* (1870). It is thought that the overall scheme was inspired by Japanese art. The particular shade of dark blue-green of the binding was adopted by many of Rossetti's associates and followers—among them Morris, Swinburne, Walter Pater, and Arthur Symons—for their own books.

56. Sir Edward Burne-Jones (1833–1898). *St. Barbara*. Gouache drawing, ca. 1865–70. (Lent by William B. O'Neal)

At Oxford, where he also met his lifelong friend William Morris, Edward Burne-Jones decided to become an artist after seeing one of Rossetti's paintings. He began as Rossetti's first pupil but later followed the advice of John Ruskin and made several visits to Italy in the 1860s. By 1870 he had turned away from Rossetti's romantic medievalism to develop his own style, which was deeply influenced by Greek and Renaissance art (especially the work of Michelangelo and Botticelli). From 1877 on, after his first exhibition at the Grosvenor Gallery (which had opened as an alternative to the Royal Academy), Burne-Jones was recognized as perhaps the most important Aesthetic painter in England. His definition of art, as he once stated it, embodied the ideals of the Aesthetic movement in general: "I mean by a picture a beautiful romantic dream of something that never was, never will be—in a light better than any light that ever shone—in a land no one can define or remember, only desire—and the forms divinely beautiful."

57. Sir Edward Burne-Jones. *Study of an Acanthus Leaf*. Pencil drawing heightened with white, after 1865. (Lent by William B. O'Neal)

Burne-Jones was one of the founders of the decorating firm started by William Morris in 1861. Over the next thirty-five years he designed for Morris and Company a bewildering number of ceramics, tapestries, and stained-glass windows. This sketch, possibly a copy of details from an architectural frieze, was probably made for some decorative work. In its naturalistic use of a plant form, it shows a remarkable affinity with Morris's own textiles and wallpapers.

58. George Howard, ninth earl of Carlisle (1843–1911). *Portrait of Edward Burne-Jones*. Pencil drawing, ca. 1885. (Lent anonymously)

An amateur painter and a patron of the arts, George Howard was friendly with many of the leading figures of his day, among them Browning, Tennyson, Frederic Leighton, and Burne-Jones. In his political views he was, though not a socialist himself, sympathetic toward William Morris. His wife, Rosalind Howard, was an early supporter of both the temperance and the women's suffrage campaigns.

59. [Barbara Leighton]. Photograph of Sir Edward Burne-Jones. Platinum print, London, 1890. (Lent anonymously)

Burne-Jones is seen in his studio, where he is at work on *The Star of Bethlehem*, a large watercolor commissioned by the city of Birmingham and completed in 1891.

60. Ford Madox Brown (1821–1893). *Study of a Draped Figure*. Black chalk drawing. (Lent by William B. O'Neal)

Ford Madox Brown belonged to an older generation of artists but was still very active in the 1880s, when he concentrated his energies on a large scheme of mural decorations for Manchester Town Hall. In 1874 his daughter married William Michael Rossetti, cementing Brown's link with the Pre-Raphaelite inner circle.

61. Sir Edward Poynter (1836–1919). *Minerva*. Crayon drawing on pink paper, 1886. (Lent by William B. O'Neal.) See fig. 7.

Edward Poynter was Burne-Jones's brother-in-law; like his more celebrated relation, he specialized in paintings with subjects drawn from Greek and Roman legends and from medieval romances. During the 1880s his work gained in both size and stature. An Aesthete but never a rebel, Poynter was also a historian of Italian art who served successively as director of the National Gallery and as president of the Royal Academy.

62. Simeon Solomon (1840–1905). *High Priest* (also called *King Solomon*). Watercolor and gouache, 1874. (Lent by William B. O'Neal)

Simeon Solomon, who was influenced by Rossetti and Burne-

7.   Sir Edward Poynter, *Minerva*, drawing (item 61)

Jones, was considered the enfant terrible of the second generation of Pre-Raphaelite artists. He was very closely associated with Swinburne and Pater until, in 1873, he was arrested on a morals charge and became a social outcast. Most of Solomon's work was inspired by biblical stories or Greek legends; but after his downfall he turned to potboilers that were among the earliest, though not the most accomplished, examples of English Symbolism. Unable or unwilling to give up his bohemian existence, Solomon was never readmitted to respectable art circles. He died in 1905, of an illness brought on by chronic alcoholism, in a London workhouse.

63. Frederic, Lord Leighton (1830–1896). *Study of Drapery*. Black chalk drawing heightened with white, ca. 1860–64. (Lent by William B. O'Neal)

Frederic Leighton's London house, with its Arab Hall decorated with Near Eastern tiles and with its collection of works by Burne-Jones, Walter Crane, and William De Morgan, was a meeting place in the 1880s for writers, musicians, and artists. Leighton himself was the leading neoclassical painter in Victorian England. In 1878 he became president of the Royal Academy; in 1896 he was given a peerage. Thus, he represented an important link between the more rebellious Aesthetic factions and the social and artistic establishments.

This drawing is of one of the foolish virgins for his *The Wise and Foolish Virgins*, a fresco painted for St. Michael's Church, Lyndhurst, in 1862–64.

64. Sir Lawrence Alma-Tadema (1836–1912). *A Dance in Spring*. Pencil drawing, ca. 1885. (Lent by William B. O'Neal.) See fig. 8.

Born in Holland, Lawrence Alma-Tadema came to settle permanently in London in 1870. He was an extremely popular painter who worked almost entirely within one genre—what has been called "Victorians in Togas"—producing pictures, based on Greek and Roman subjects, that were accurate in their renderings of classical architecture but in every other way anachronistic. His kind of Aestheticism proved irresistible to late Victorian contemporaries who wanted to escape further back than the medieval or Renaissance periods. This drawing, inscribed by the artist to his friend David Murray, the Scottish landscape painter, is thought to be a study for a larger work.

65. George Frederic Watts (1817–1904). *When the Earth Was Young*. Oil on canvas, ca. 1875–90. (Lent by University of Virginia Art Museum)

8. Sir Lawrence Alma-Tadema, *A Dance in Spring*,
drawing (item 64)

This painting probably is related to the series of works that George Frederic Watts called *The House of Life,* each picture of which captures a different symbolic moment in history. In size and style it is similar to *The Creation of Eve* (ca. 1890) in the Lady Lever Art Gallery, Port Sunlight.

66. George Frederic Watts. *Head of a Woman.* Black and white chalk drawing, ca. 1860–70. (Lent by William B. O'Neal)
    Watts wanted to be thought of as an intellectual painter of serious, often allegorical, subjects. His real fame, however, grew from the long series of portraits he did of eminent men and women. By the 1890s his sitters included Arnold, Tennyson, Morris, Burne-Jones, George Meredith, Frederic Leighton, and Josephine Butler, the crusader for women's rights.

67. John Roddam Spencer Stanhope (1839–1908). *Night* (also called *Evening*). Oil on canvas, 1878. (Lent by University of Virginia Art Museum)
    A student of Watts, J. R. Spencer Stanhope was one of the leaders of the second generation of Pre-Raphaelite artists. His allegorical and mythological subjects were exhibited widely, both at the Royal Academy and at the "antiestablishment" Grosvenor Gallery. In 1880 he settled permanently in Florence, where he was joined at the turn of the century by his niece and pupil, Evelyn De Morgan, and her husband, William De Morgan, the potter. Much of Spencer Stanhope's art was inspired by the work of Burne-Jones; this painting very probably derives from an 1870 watercolor by Burne-Jones of the same subject (now in the Fogg Museum, Harvard University).

 William Morris and His Associates

68. William Morris (1834–1896). *Brother Rabbit.* Printed textile, designed in 1883. (Lent anonymously)
    Between 1864 and the end of his life, William Morris designed more than eighty patterns for textiles and wallpapers. His prolific output was at its peak in the mid-1880s, also the time of his deepest involvement with socialist politics.

69. William Morris. *Rose.* Printed textile, designed in 1883. (Lent anonymously)
    This pattern apparently was inspired by a sixteenth-century brocade which Morris saw in the South Kensington Museum (now the Victoria and Albert Museum).

70. [Morris and Company?]. Teapot, cup, bowl, and creamer. Painted earthenware, ca. 1879. (Lent anonymously)

Though not, like Rossetti or Whistler, a collector of blue-and-white china, Morris was not immune to its charm or influence. He is believed to have designed these dishes in 1879 as a wedding present for Joseph Jacobs (1854–1916), the English fairy-tale writer and folklorist; certainly, the stylized repeat pattern of the flowers is typical of Morris's work. The large, handleless cup is of the type preferred by Morris for his own use as a coffee mug. It is similar to one in the William Morris Gallery, London.

71. William De Morgan (1839–1917). Decorative tile. Painted earthenware, ca. 1885–90. (Lent by William B. O'Neal)

An associate of Morris, William De Morgan was the foremost potter of the Aesthetic movement. In 1881 he moved his factory from London to Merton Abbey, Surrey, to be near Morris's works. His designs often were modeled on Near Eastern ceramics, and he was responsible for the installation of the famous Arab Hall in the house of Frederic, Lord Leighton. After his business failed in 1905 De Morgan turned to the writing of heavily plotted, Dickensian novels, achieving fame and fortune with his first effort, *Joseph Vance: An Ill-written Autobiography* (1906).

72. William Morris. *The Decorative Arts: Their Relation to Modern Life and Progress*. London, [1878].

In a letter of 5 September 1883 to Andreas Scheu, an Austrian-born socialist, Morris explained the cause of his opposition to pure Aestheticism and his reasons for combining the decorative arts with politics:

Almost all the designs we use [at "The Firm"] for surface decoration, wallpapers, textiles, and the like, I design myself. I have had to learn the theory and to some extent the practice of weaving, dyeing, & textile printing: all of which I must admit has given me and still gives me a great deal of enjoyment.

But in spite of all the success I have had, I have not failed to be conscious that the art I have been helping to produce would fall with the death of the few of us who really care about it, that a reform in art which is founded on individualism must perish with the individuals who have set it going. Both my historical studies and my practical conflict with the philistinism of modern society have *forced* on me the conviction that art cannot have a real life and growth under the present system of commercialism and profit-mongering. I have tried to develop this view, which is in fact Socialism seen through the eyes of an artist, in various lectures, the first of which I delivered in 1878.

73. Moncure Daniel Conway (1832–1907). *Travels in South Kensington.* London, 1882. See figs. 9 and 10.

Moncure Daniel Conway, a Virginia-born abolitionist and free-thinker, moved in 1863 to London, where he became the minister of the South Place Unitarian Church. He was closely connected with the Pre-Raphaelite artists and acted as a link between English and American writers (he helped to bring about the first publication of Walt Whitman's poems in England in 1868 and later wrote a book on Carlyle for the American audience).

Conway's *Travels in South Kensington* is one of the key documents of the Aesthetic movement. Its three chapters deal with the South Kensington (now the Victoria and Albert) Museum; with Bedford Park, the first "garden suburb" specially developed by and for artists in 1875, where Conway himself lived; and with the current state of the decorative arts in England. Not surprisingly, Conway devoted much attention to the work of his friend William Morris. In his later *Autobiography* (1904), Conway would both defend Morris's reputation and define his anomalous position as a gentleman socialist:

> Again and again have I stood in Hyde Park with the humble crowd listening to William Morris, while carriages of the wealthy rolled past. He too might have enjoyed his carriage . . . [but instead] a rude bench for his pulpit, rough people for his audience, William Morris raged against himself as one of the class of their non-producing oppressors. 'If I were in the situation of most of you I should take to hard drinking. . . .'
>
> William Morris impressed me then as a noble but still more a pathetic figure. . . . For I believe his premature death was in part due to disillusion . . . as one who spoke to the multitudes in an unknown tongue, as if Prospero had called up his exquisite masque for a company of comparative Calibans.

74. William Morris. *The Odyssey of Homer Done into English Verse.* 2 vols. London, 1887.

Morris was as prolific a translator as he was a prose writer, lecturer, poet, designer, and printer. This verse translation of Homer's epic followed Morris's own versions of the *Aeneid* (1876) and of many Icelandic sagas (done in collaboration with Eirikr Magnusson), and it preceded his *Beowulf* (1895).

75. William Morris. *Signs of Change: Seven Lectures Delivered on Various Occasions.* London, 1888.

9.   Moncure D. Conway, *Travels in South Kensington*
(London, 1882), illustration depicting the drawing
room at Bellevue House, William Bell Scott's
residence (item 73)

10.   Moncure D. Conway, *Travels in South Kensington*
(London, 1882), illustration reproducing a portrait of
William Morris (item 73)

Morris's active involvement with radical politics came to a head in the late 1880s. On 13 November 1887, known afterwards as "Bloody Sunday," the police used violent means to break up a socialist demonstration in Trafalgar Square. At a similar protest on the following Sunday, a man named Alfred Linnell was fatally injured; Morris delivered an address at his funeral. In 1888, as part of his continuing public efforts on behalf of reform, Morris issued this volume of political speeches and writings. The title, *Signs of Change*, showed his unflagging optimism even in a time of crisis. This copy of the book belonged to Morris's friend George P. Boyce (1826–1897), the watercolor painter.

76. William Morris. *A Dream of John Ball*. Autograph manuscript (see fig. 11). 1st ed., London, 1888. (Lent anonymously.) Kelmscott Press ed., [London], 1892.

A *Dream of John Ball* was Morris's way of clothing political rhetoric in the garb of romance. A fantasy or "vision" based on Wat Tyler's rebellion against Richard II in the fourteenth century, it served as a link between Morris's socialist lectures of the 1880s and his prose tales of the 1890s—beginning with *News from Nowhere* and continuing through *The Well at the World's End* and others to *The Sundering Flood*—in which he increasingly let his imagination run free.

The story first appeared in installments in the *Commonweal*, the organ of the Socialist League sponsored by Morris, from November 1886 to January 1887. It was published, together with the shorter "A King's Lesson," as a book in 1888 with an etched frontispiece after a design by Burne-Jones. With the text slightly revised, *A Dream of John Ball* was reprinted in 1892 as the sixth book issued by Morris's own Kelmscott Press, a venture which Morris had begun in 1891 "with the hope of producing some [books] which would have a definite claim to beauty." In the Kelmscott edition the Burne-Jones etching was replaced by a woodcut.

The original autograph manuscript is signed at the end by the author and bound in vellum by the Kelmscott Press's bindery. Morris's own copy of the Kelmscott edition, one of eleven copies printed on vellum, has his bookplate and a clipped autograph signature. The copy of the ordinary Kelmscott issue of three hundred on paper was presented by Morris to William Harcourt Hooper, the engraver of the frontispiece by Burne-Jones and of most of the illustrations in other Kelmscott Press books.

77. William Morris. *News from Nowhere: or An Epoch of Rest, Being Some Chapters from a Utopian Romance*. London, 1891.

— A Dream of John Ball —

11. William Morris, *A Dream of John Ball*, first
page of the autograph manuscript (item 76)

In the 16 June 1894 issue of the socialist journal *Justice*, Morris defined socialism as "a condition of society in which there should be neither rich nor poor, neither master nor master's man, neither idle nor overworked, neither brain-sick brain workers, nor heart-sick hand workers, in a word, in which all men would be living in equality of condition . . . the realization at last of the meaning of the word COMMONWEALTH." *News from Nowhere*, which appeared serially in the *Commonweal* in 1890, was Morris's utopian fantasy of life in such a commonwealth. Its setting is an England of the future, in which not only economic and political equality but also equality of the sexes had been achieved. This is one of the 250 large-paper copies of the first English book edition.

 Algernon Charles Swinburne

78. William Bell Scott (1811–1890). *Portrait of A. C. Swinburne*. Etching proof, 1860. (Lent by Cecil Y. Lang)

Much like his friend D. G. Rossetti, William Bell Scott was both a poet and a painter. This etching is a miniature version of Scott's oil portrait, now at Balliol College, Oxford, of the young Algernon Charles Swinburne, whom Scott had met as early as 1857. At this time Swinburne was known only as a precocious Oxford dropout; his first book, *The Queen Mother. Rosamond*, published later in 1860, attracted little attention. Not until the appearance of *Poems and Ballads* in 1866 did the flamboyant poet gain his notoriety.

79. Algernon Charles Swinburne (1837–1909). Autograph letter signed to Arthur Henry Bullen (1857–1920), 18 May 1886.

In this letter to Arthur Henry Bullen, a Shakespearean scholar, Swinburne maliciously quoted extracts from the poetry of an untalented American writer as examples of "nobly unconscious burlesque" in literature:

> I fear you must be capable of preferring Longfellow to the one truly great Bard of America—Dr. Thomas H. Chivers. As it is just possible you may not be deeply read in the lyric work of that immortal man (though a copy of his 'Virginalia: or, Visions of my Summer Nights'—also published, I believe, under the yet lovelier title of 'Phials of Amber for the Tears of the Beautiful'—is in the library of the British Museum, where I read it many years ago—disturbing, I fear, my neighbours by hardly suppressible explosions of laughter) I send you a sample. . . . I really prefer this writer to Horace. And so I fancy would you if you had been so pestered with Horace from twelve to sixteen as I was.

80. Algernon Charles Swinburne. *A Word for the Navy*. London, 1887.
(Lent anonymously)

Swinburne's poem for Queen Victoria's Jubilee was published by George Redway, a wily bookseller who had received the copyright in exchange for returning to the poet a group of potentially embarrassing letters. It first appeared in Redway's 1887 anthology *Sea Song and River Rhyme*, then was quickly reprinted in a pamphlet limited to 250 copies. Swinburne presented this copy to John Nichol (1833–1894), a friend from his Oxford days who had become professor of English at the University of Glasgow.

81. Ape [Carlo Pellegrini]. *Before Sunrise: Algernon Charles Swinburne*. Color lithograph, published in *Vanity Fair*, 21 November 1874. (Lent by Cecil Y. Lang)

Edmund Gosse once owned the original drawing for this caricature and wrote of it, "Although avowedly a caricature, this is in many ways the best surviving record of Swinburne's general aspect and attitude." The title refers to Swinburne's volume *Songs Before Sunrise* (1871), in which the poet praised both republicanism (it was dedicated to "Joseph Mazzini," the Italian revolutionary) and the work of Walt Whitman.

82. Algernon Charles Swinburne. Autograph letter signed to the editor of the *Academy*, 2 July 1880.

This letter, which the editor to whom Swinburne addressed it, James Sutherland Cotton (1847–1918), refused to publish, formed part of the long-lived quarrel between Swinburne and Frederick J. Furnivall, founder of the Browning and Shelley societies. In 1873 Furnivall had established the New Shakespeare Society, the work of which Swinburne attacked in a series of articles collected in *A Study of Shakespeare* (1880). The publication of the book led to a barrage of angry letters to the press and eventually to the printing of Furnivall's notorious pamphlet, *The Co. of Pigsbrook & Co.* [1881], a vicious defamation of Swinburne in which the poet was labeled a "drunken clown" (after Furnivall called Swinburne "Pigsbrook," the latter responded by turning his antagonist's name into the appropriate Anglo-Saxonism, "Brothelsdyke").

Swinburne's friend and biographer, Edmund Gosse, preserved this letter in his copy of *A Study of Shakespeare*.

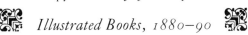 *Illustrated Books, 1880–90*

The high Aesthetic style of book design and illustration in the 1880s was less an example of innovation than of recombination, a mode dependent upon borrowings from the past and from abroad. In these volumes, many of them books for children—who would, it was hoped, grow up to be Aesthetes rather than Philistines—one can see the effects of everything from the Queen Anne revival and the later Pre-Raphaelite movement to the importation of blue-and-white porcelain from Japan. Some of the hallmarks of Aesthetic illustration were imitation eighteenth-century or Regency dress, figures of languid ladies, and an emphasis upon flowers—particularly sunflowers, which would become the emblem of Oscar Wilde and his followers. Also common to these designers, some of whom were writers as well, was a high degree of wit and even of self-parody, as may be seen in the binding for *The Baby's Opera*, where the long-beaked bird represents his creator, the artist Walter Crane.

83. Francis William Bourdillon (1852–1921). *Young Maids and Old China*. London, [1889].

The illustrations by John G. Sowerby (fl. 1876–1925) are extremely reminiscent of the work of Walter Crane. The text is by Francis William Bourdillon, a minor poet in an era of minor poets, who is remembered today only for a single line—"The night has a thousand eyes"—from a poem published in his first book, *Among the Flowers, and Other Poems* (1878).

84. Randolph Caldecott (1846–1886). *Graphic Pictures*. London, 1883.

This is the oversized and brilliantly colored omnibus volume of Randolph Caldecott's contributions to the weekly *Graphic* magazine.

85. Kate Greenaway (1846–1901). *Under the Window*. New York, 1880.

First published in London in 1878, this book immediately raised Kate Greenaway to fame. John Ruskin singled her out for praise in *The Art of England* (1884), while nevertheless warning her not to use her talents "merely for illumination": "Miss Greenaway has been wasting her strength too sorrowfully in making the edges of her little birthday books, and the like, glitter with unregarded gold, whereas her power should be concentrated in the direct illustration of connected story, and her pictures should be made complete on the page, and far more realistic than decorative." Greenaway, however, continued to work in a purely Aesthetic mode, producing highly stylized drawings that owed much to Walter Crane's example, especially in their evocations of nostalgia for eighteenth-century rural life.

This copy is probably the first American edition.

86. Kate Greenaway. *The Language of Flowers*. London, 1884.

87. Walter Crane (1845–1915). *The Baby's Opera*. 1st American ed. New York, [1877].

    After William Morris, Walter Crane was the most versatile and prolific artist associated with the Aesthetic movement. Painter, wood engraver, designer of textiles and ceramics, poet, socialist, and writer on art, he served twice as president of the Arts and Crafts Exhibition Society and helped found the Art Workers Guild. To the middle classes, however, Crane was known as the illustrator of children's books by such authors as Nathaniel Hawthorne, Mrs. Molesworth, and the brothers Grimm. In the mid-1860s he began his own series of toy books—little volumes bound in wrappers or pictorial boards, priced at sixpence or a shilling, and actually meant to be read by children—which culminated in *The Baby's Opera, The Baby's Bouquet* (1879), and *Baby's Own Aesop* (1886). In producing these and other works with conscious echoes of Japanese and Greek art, Crane's aim was to provide "good art in the nursery"; as he explained in *Of the Decorative Illustration of Books* (1896), "In a sober and matter-of-fact age they afford perhaps the only outlet for unrestricted flights of fancy open to the modern illustrator."

88. [John Richard de Capel Wise (1831–1890)]. *The First of May, a Fairy Masque*. Boston, 1881.

    A cousin of J. A. Froude and an early disciple of both J. S. Mill and Herbert Spencer, John Richard de Capel Wise was also a scholar, a naturalist, and a poet. His *The New Forest* (1863), long the standard book on that part of the English countryside, contained Walter Crane's first published illustrations. When Wise inherited a fortune in 1878, he commissioned Crane to provide the artwork for *The First of May*, an elaborate gift book which he arranged to issue through Sotheran, the bookseller. Although relatively unknown today, due to the small editions printed—this is one of only two hundred proof copies signed by Crane—*The First of May* reproduces a very fine series of designs that combine many of the whimsical and retrospective elements of Aesthetic art.

89. *Living English Poets MDCCCLXXXII*. London, 1883. (Lent anonymously.) See fig. 12.

    For this anonymously edited anthology, Walter Crane provided a frontispiece which was unexpectedly satirical. Shown in front of a Greek-robed and Pre-Raphaelite-coifed muse of poetry are some of the "living English poets" who contributed to the volume, each

12. *Living English Poets MDCCCXXXII* (London,
1882), frontispiece by Walter Crane (item 89)

holding his most famous work. The portraits of Swinburne, Browning, Arnold, and Tennyson are recognizable caricatures, but the one of William Morris, whose socialist views were shared wholeheartedly by Crane, is almost a travesty. This copy of *Living English Poets* appears to have been bound specially in parchment and is from the library of Christina Rossetti, who contributed eight poems.

90. Andrew Lang (1844–1912). *XXXII Ballades in Blue China.* London, 1881.
   The designer of this volume remains unidentified, but the frontispiece and title page reflect the author's own Francophile Aestheticism.

91. William Allingham (1824–1889). *Rhymes for the Young Folk.* London, [1886]. (Lent anonymously.) See fig. 13.
   William Allingham is chiefly remembered now for a single poem, "The Fairies" ("Up the airy mountain, / Down the rushy glen . . ."), and for his lengthy *Diary,* which was published posthumously in 1907 and records in detail conversations with Carlyle, Tennyson, and various Pre-Raphaelites. This charming collection of poems for children contains illustrations by Kate Greenaway and by Harry Furniss (1854–1925), known for his drawings for Lewis Carroll's *Sylvie and Bruno* (1889); but it is really an Allingham family production. Most of the artwork is by the author's wife, Helen Allingham (1848–1926), a talented watercolorist who also illustrated Thomas Hardy's *Far from the Madding Crowd* (1874), and by her sister, Caroline Paterson. Allingham himself did two of the drawings and is depicted in several others, including one which shows him introducing his eldest son, Gerald, to "one of the fairies." Like many of the books illustrated by Greenaway and Crane, *Rhymes for the Young Folk* was printed by Edmund Evans, the acknowledged master of Victorian color reproduction.

92. Henry Ryland (1856–1924). Decorative tile. Painted earthenware, ca. 1879. (Lent anonymously.) See fig. 14.
   The eclectic and fanciful style of Aesthetic book illustration was soon picked up by designers of decorative objects. Henry Ryland, who began his career as a studio assistant to Burne-Jones, managed in this tile to add the note of Kate Greenaway's childlike simplicity to what has been called his usual "sugary combination of Alma-Tadema and Albert Moore." This tile is one of a pair presented by Burne-Jones to the writer Joseph Jacobs on the occasion of the latter's marriage in 1879.

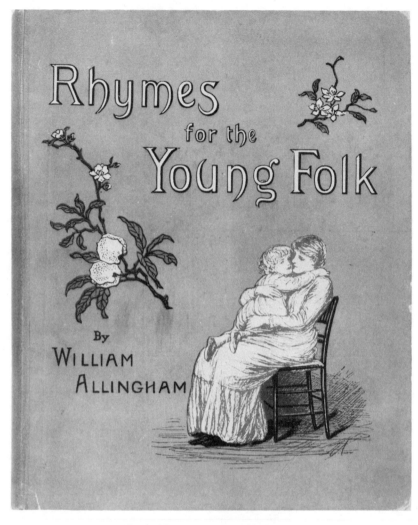

13.   William Allingham, *Rhymes for the Young Folk*
(London, [1886]), front cover design by Helen
Allingham (item 91)

14. Henry Ryland, decorative tile (item 92)

Walter Pater and His Circle

93. Walter Horatio Pater (1839–1894). *Studies in the History of the Renaissance*. London, 1873.

The central document of the Aesthetic movement was not produced by the flamboyant painter J. M. Whistler or the self-publicizing Oscar Wilde, but by a fastidious and retiring Oxford don, who was appalled by the stir that his "Conclusion," the last chapter of a book of art criticism, caused. Indeed, in 1877 he removed the offending chapter from the second edition of the work, so as to discourage public identification between his own philosophy and the excesses of his more outrageous disciples. The damage, however, was done. The "Conclusion" remained, in the eyes of Walter Pater's supporters and detractors alike, a manifesto for hedonism and amoral Aestheticism—the source of the injunction to "burn always with this hard gemlike flame," the observation that "Not the fruit of experience, but experience itself is the end" of life, and, most important, the phrase "love of art for art's sake," which became the Aesthetes' slogan. Even with these passages excised, *The Renaissance* still offered much inspiration for the eager young apostles of beauty. In Pater's rhapsody upon Leonardo da Vinci's painting *La Gioconda* (also known as the Mona Lisa), for instance, they found the height of impressionistic criticism and beautiful style taking precedence over intellectual or moral content:

> Here is the head upon which all 'the ends of the world are come,' and the eyelids are a little weary. . . . She is older than the rocks among which she sits; like the vampire, she has been dead many times, and learned the secrets of the grave; and has been a diver in deep seas, and keeps their fallen day about her . . . and all this has been to her but as the sound of lyres and flutes, and lives only in the delicacy with which it has moulded the changing lineaments and tinged the eyelids and the hands.

94. Walter Pater. *Marius the Epicurean: His Sensations and Ideas*. 2 vols. London, 1885.

In his "Conclusion" to *The Renaissance*, Pater had expressed his sense of the fleetingness of life and urged his audience to "catch at any exquisite passion . . . or any stirring of the senses, strange dyes, strange flowers, and curious odours, or work of the artist's hands." Readers who knew Pater only through this bit of prose expected the author to be a reckless bohemian, living out his carpe diem philosophy in a mad pursuit of new experiences. But as Thomas Hardy noted after meeting him in 1886, the "real" Pater was a man "whose

manner is that of one carrying weighty ideas without spilling them."
Indeed, he had more in common with the grave Victorian moralists,
such as Matthew Arnold, than his followers liked to admit. In
Marius the Epicurean, his historical novel set in the Rome of Marcus
Aurelius, he qualified his earlier position. It was not hedonism that
he was advocating but a disciplined and demanding education both of
the senses and of the intellect. For Pater, the training of an Aesthete
was akin to that of a priest, requiring patience, dedication, and self-
sacrifice.

95. Sir Max Beerbohm (1872–1956). *Oxford 1891: Mr. Walter Pater
Taking His Walk through the Meadows.* Pencil and watercolor, 1928.
(Lent anonymously)

In "Diminuendo," a comic essay published in *The Works of Max
Beerbohm* (1896), Beerbohm gave the following account of a memorable moment during his undergraduate days at Oxford:

> I remember how my tutor asked me what lectures I wished to attend,
> and how he laughed when I said I wished to attend the lectures of Mr.
> Walter Pater. . . . one morning soon after, I went to Ryman's to
> order some foolish engraving . . . and there saw . . . a small, thick,
> rock-faced man, whose top-hat and gloves of *bright* dog-skin struck
> one of the many discords in that little city of learning or laughter. The
> serried bristles of his mustachio made for him a false-military air. I
> think I nearly went down when they told me that this was Pater.

96. Walter Pater. *An Imaginary Portrait*. Oxford: Daniel Press, 1894.

Unlike Pater's other exercises in verbal portraiture, the story
called "The Child in the House" was in fact purely a self-portrait, an
evocation of sensations recalled from the author's melancholy boyhood. Through the medium of fiction, Pater was able to discover and
recover the early blossomings of his own Aesthetic temperament—
especially, his painfully acute responses to beauty, loss, and death—
here attributed, however, to the "imaginary" child, Florian Deleal.

First published in *Macmillan's Magazine* in August 1878, the
story was reprinted separately, with Pater's permission and revisions,
in this pamphlet issued by the Daniel Press for a charity fête. It did
not appear in the volume titled *Imaginary Portraits* (1887).

97. Walter Pater. *Essays from* The Guardian. [London], 1896.

This privately printed volume was edited anonymously by Edmund Gosse. In the preface, he described the circumstances of its
issue: "It has been discovered, through the kindness of the present
editor of the 'Guardian,' Mr. D. C. Lathbury, that Walter Pater

contributed to the pages of that newspaper nine anonymous articles. . . . it has been thought worth while to preserve these . . .
although their positive value may be slight. They are crumbs from
the table of his delicate and never copious feast, and it is to the inner
circle of his friends that they are here offered." Among the essays
reprinted are reviews of Arthur Symons's *An Introduction to the Study
of Browning,* Mrs. Humphry Ward's *Robert Elsmere,* and Gosse's
own *On Viol and Flute.*

Gosse inscribed this copy to Henry James, a sometimes ambivalent
member of the "inner circle" of Pater's admirers.

98. Sir Max Beerbohm. *Mr. Gosse and the Rising Generation.* Pencil and
watercolor, ca. 1910. (Lent anonymously)

While a young assistant in the British Museum, Edmund Gosse
was taken up by several established artists and writers, including
Rossetti and Swinburne. When he in turn rose to fame, particularly
after his appointment as librarian to the House of Lords in 1904,
Gosse became a nurturer and defender of the "rising generation."
His protégés included Max Beerbohm, E. M. Forster, Charlotte
Mew, and Siegfried Sassoon.

99. Sir Edmund Gosse (1849–1928). *On Viol and Flute.* New York,
1886.

Like many literary Englishmen, Gosse found the United States a
friendly and lucrative place in which to give lectures. His first tour,
which lasted from 1884 to 1885, brought him the friendship of
many American authors, including Oliver Wendell Holmes, Whitman, Howells, and E. C. Stedman. The success of his lectures led to
his being offered a chair at Johns Hopkins and to the publication of
this volume, which was composed of selections from his English
books of verse.

100. [Sir Edmund Gosse]. *Father and Son: A Study of Two Temperaments.*
London, 1907.

For many Aesthetes of the 1880s the pursuit of beauty represented
their rebellion not merely against middle-class society in general but
against their own families in particular, and especially against their
fathers. The younger Gosse paid his official tribute to his father, a
famous marine zoologist, in a biography finished in 1890, two years
after Philip Henry Gosse's death. But the unofficial account of how
Philip Henry, a religious zealot, had bullied and terrorized his son,
isolating him from other children, prohibiting him from reading
storybooks or other "lies" of art, and forcing him to dedicate himself
to God, forms the more interesting subject matter of this book,

which was published anonymously. The conclusion to Edmund Gosse's "study" of the formation of his own artistic temperament sums up the experiences through which many of his Aesthetic contemporaries passed on their way to embracing art as their religion:

> Then came a moment when my self-sufficiency revolted against the police inspection to which my 'views' were incessantly subjected. . . .
>
> All that I need further say is to point out that when such defiance is offered to the intelligence of a thoughtful and honest young man with the normal impulses of his twenty-one years, there are but two alternatives. Either he must cease to think for himself; or his individualism must be instantly confirmed . . . and thus desperately challenged, the young man's conscience threw off once for all the yoke of his 'dedication,' and, as respectfully as he could, without parade or remonstrance, he took a human being's privilege to fashion his inner life for himself.

101. Henry James (1843–1916). *Partial Portraits*. London, 1888.

The long friendship between Edmund Gosse and Henry James began with their introduction in 1879 at a luncheon at which R. L. Stevenson and Andrew Lang were also present. For Gosse, a collector of literary and social lions, James was a prize catch who could lead him to other trophies; as he recalled after a later meeting, "James talked with increasing ease, but always with a punctilious hesitancy, about Paris, where he seemed, to my dazzlement, to know even a larger number of persons of distinction than he did in London." Among the figures whom Gosse met through James was Guy de Maupassant, the subject of one of the critical essays collected in *Partial Portraits*. Another "portrait" was a study of the English illustrator George Du Maurier, with whom both James and Gosse socialized.

In the essay on Du Maurier, James announced, perhaps a bit prematurely, the death of the Aesthetic movement: "The new aesthetic life, in short, shows signs of drawing to a close, after having, as many people tell us, effected a revolution in English taste—having at least, if not peopled the land with beauty, made certain consecrated forms of ugliness henceforth impossible." But the chief fame of *Partial Portraits* lies in its being the volume in which James's great essay on novel writing, "The Art of Fiction" (first published in *Longman's Magazine*, September 1884) was collected.

This copy was presented by Henry James to Edmund Gosse.

102. Elliott and Fry. Photograph of Henry James. Albumen or silver print, London, ca. 1890–95.

The photograph is inscribed "Yours till death" and signed by Henry James.

103. Vernon Lee [Violet Paget (1856–1935)]. *Miss Brown: A Novel.* 3 vols. Edinburgh, 1884.

When Violet Paget, the essayist and novelist whose unconventional life in Florence shocked many and whose affectation of masculine guise went beyond the use of a male pseudonym, dedicated this roman à clef about the world of the Aesthetes to Henry James, the latter was sorely embarrassed. He complained in a letter of 12 December 1884 to Thomas Sergeant Perry: "As I told you, my modest name is on the dedication-page, and my tongue is therefore tied in speaking of it—at least generally. But I may whisper in your ear that as it is her first attempt at a novel, so it is to be hoped that it may be her last. . . . It is in short a rather deplorable mistake—to be repented of. But I am afraid she won't repent—it's not her line."

104. Vernon Lee [Violet Paget]. Autograph letter signed to John H. Ingram (1849–1916), 22 June [1884].

John H. Ingram, better known as an early biographer of Edgar Allan Poe, was also editor of the Eminent Women Series, in which Violet Paget published her biography, *The Countess of Albany* (1884). Evidently the path to publication was not smooth, for she wrote to Ingram:

> I have returned the last batch of the proofsheets which, by the way, far surpass my wildest imagination in the way of disgraceful printing, to Messrs. Allen. . . . With regard to my delaying the publication, pray bear in mind that I let you have the MS. several days before the appointed date, and that two months delay in going to press cannot always be compensated by overloading an author with more proofsheets than can be corrected at a sitting. . . . It is my interest as well as yours that the book be soon out, and it won't be a bit quicker for bothering me about it.

105. Vernon Lee [Violet Paget]. *Euphorion: Being Studies of the Antique and the Medieval in the Renaissance.* 2 vols. London, 1884.

Violet Paget was among the few women of the day to express her rebellion against Victorian values through devotion not to social causes but to artistic ones—particularly to the Aesthetic principles of her mentor, Walter Pater. In 1881, while visiting Oxford with her beloved friend Mary Robinson, she first met Pater and his sisters at the house of Mrs. Humphry Ward. *Euphorion* was her own version of *Studies in the History of the Renaissance*, a collection of essays written between 1882 and 1884 on subjects such as the treatment of Italy in Elizabethan drama, Renaissance portrait art, and courtly love.

Unlike Henry James, who was so dismayed by the dedication to him of *Miss Brown*, Pater was honored by the compliment she paid him in *Euphorion*. As he wrote to her on 4 June 1884, "*Euphorion* arrived last Saturday. It is a very great pleasure to me to find myself associated with literary work so delightful and so excellent as yours, and I thank you sincerely for your generous and graceful dedication to myself." This copy belonged to Paget's and James's friend, John Singer Sargent (1856–1925), the American expatriate painter, who had done an oil sketch of her in 1881.

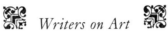 *Writers on Art*

106. Mrs. H. R. [Mary Eliza] Haweis (1852–1898). *The Art of Decoration*. London, 1889. (Lent by the Fiske-Kimball Fine Arts Library)

How-to books were a profitable feature of the Aesthetic movement. Aimed primarily at the upper-middle classes who could afford to build houses filled with collectibles, these guides defined taste by giving specific and eclectic examples of what artistically minded readers should buy. Mrs. H. R. Haweis, the wife of a liberal cleric who was friendly with Oscar Wilde and the Rossettis, was possibly the most prolific author in this genre. An earlier work, *Beautiful Houses* (1881), was a travelogue through artists' studios and country estates. *The Art of Decoration*, which has chapters on "The Queen Anne Style" and "Roman Ornament," provided not only a critical history of style but precise recommendations for walls, windows, lighting, and movables.

107. Walter Hamilton (1844–1899). *The Aesthetic Movement in England*. London, 1882. (Lent by the Fiske-Kimball Fine Arts Library)

Written in response to the jibes of *Punch*, Gilbert and Sullivan's *Patience*, and the now forgotten play *The Colonel* (1881) by F. C. Burnand, this work by Walter Hamilton was the first serious study of Aestheticism. Its contents outline the development of the "Aesthetic school" from the Pre-Raphaelites to Oscar Wilde. Among the writers considered are Ruskin, D. G. Rossetti, Swinburne, and the minor poet Arthur O'Shaughnessy. Hamilton's definition of the Aesthetic movement was both broad and sympathetic:

> a comparatively new school, which has done, and is still doing, an immense amount of good towards the advancement of Art in this country and in America . . ., the Aesthetes are they who pride them-

selves upon having found out what is the really beautiful in nature and art. . . . having first laid down certain general principles, they have endeavored to elevate taste into a scientific system, the correlation of the arts being a main feature of the scheme. . . .

. . . the essence of the movement is the union of persons of cultivated tastes to define . . . what is to be admired.

Like almost everyone else connected with the Aesthetic revolution, Hamilton could not resist giving advice on art and the decoration of houses. Urging his readers to follow the lead of the painters who exhibited at the Grosvenor Gallery and to heed the teachings of Ruskin and Morris, he concluded the chapter titled "The Home of the Aesthetes" by admonishing: "Away with all shams; study art for art's sake; avoid false gold and pretentious glitter; adopt a simple style moulded on the forms and colours of nature."

108. *Century Guild Hobby Horse.* London, 1886–92. (Lent by the Fiske-Kimball Fine Arts Library)

The widespread excitement created by the Aesthetic movement led in the 1880s to the establishment of many new arts organizations. One of the smallest but most important was the Century Guild, founded in 1882 by Arthur H. Mackmurdo (1851–1942), the architect of the Savoy Hotel and Theater, where many of Gilbert and Sullivan's operas were first performed. Following the teachings of Ruskin and Morris, the guild endeavored "to render all branches of art the sphere no longer of the tradesman but of the artist." In the belief that literature and the fine and applied arts could not be separated, the guild started its own magazine in 1886 (a single inaugural issue in 1884 proved premature). This was the *Hobby Horse*, edited by Mackmurdo's associates Arthur Galton, Herbert P. Horne (1865–1916), and Selwyn Image (1849–1930).

With its striking cover design by Image and its elegant typography, the *Hobby Horse* had a strong influence upon Morris's Kelmscott Press productions. Equally remarkable were the magazine's literary contents, which created a link through the Aesthetic movement between the earlier Pre-Raphaelites and the Decadents of the 1890s. Among the contributors were Matthew Arnold, Oscar Wilde, J. A. Symonds, Katherine Tynan, Christina and William Rossetti, and Michael Field (Edith Cooper and Katherine Bradley).

109. John Addington Symonds (1840–1893). *Renaissance in Italy: The Age of the Despots.* 2d ed. London, 1880.

J. A. Symonds, the son of a prominent West Country doctor, devoted his life completely to the study of Aesthetic culture. He followed his brilliant career at Oxford with marriage and eventual expatriation to Switzerland and Italy; but flight from England could not free him either from the ill health that dogged him or from the torment of what he called "the problem," i.e., his homosexual inclinations.

Symonds did not wish to be considered part of the Aesthetic movement per se, but his books had a deeply felt influence on its adherents. In *Renaissance in Italy*, his magnum opus published in seven volumes between 1875 and 1886, Symonds brought together ideas expressed by Pater in *Studies in the History of the Renaissance* with others found in Darwin's *The Origin of Species*. The result was a romantic view of the Italian Renaissance as a "golden age," infused with the spirit of Greek art and poetry, but also as part of the evolutionary development of human history.

This copy of the first volume of *Renaissance in Italy* is from the library of Henry James, who, on meeting Symonds in 1877, described him as "a mild, cultured man, with the Oxford perfume."

110. John Addington Symonds. *Animi Figura*. London, 1882.

In his preface to this extended sonnet sequence, Symonds explained that "the book is meant to be what it calls itself, the Portrait of a Mind"; moreover, "the mind here figured is intended for that of an artist, as distinguished from the man of action." Typical of these musings on spiritual and aesthetic dilemma, couched in language borrowed shamelessly from Swinburne, were the following lines from the poem titled "The Pursuit of Beauty":

> So the soul, drawn by beauty, nothing loth,
> Burns her bright wings with rapture that is pain,
> Faints and dissolves or e'er her goal she gain,
> Flies and pursues that unclasped deity,
> Fretful, forestalled, blown into foam and froth,
> Following and foiled, even as I follow Thee!

This copy belonged to Henry James.

111. John Addington Symonds. Autograph letter signed to Richard Watson Gilder (1844–1909), 28 November 1881.

Richard Watson Gilder, poet and editor of the *Century*, had sent Symonds a copy of *Oldport Days* (1873) by Thomas Wentworth Higginson (1823–1911), the American clergyman and abolitionist. Symonds replied: "I turn to thank you for the very charming book 'Old port Days' which I have read through with interest & lent to my friend R. L. Stevenson (you may know some of his work 'A journey with a Donkey' 'Virginibus Puerisque' etc.)." The rest of this letter answers Gilder's questions about the Symonds family's pedigree.

❦ Oscar Wilde ❦

112. Oscar Wilde (1854–1900). *Poems*. London, 1881. (Lent anonymously)

Although his reputation now rests on his essays, plays, some short stories, and a novel, Oscar Wilde began his literary career as a poet. During his Oxford years he contributed single poems to various magazines, and in 1878 he won the Newdigate Prize with *Ravenna*. This volume, issued at the author's expense, was the first collection of his verse. Its typography and binding (a gold floral design on cream parchment) are reminiscent of Rossetti's *Poems* (1870); much of the book's contents could also be called imitative—of Rossetti, Swinburne, Morris, Arnold, and Browning.

113. George Du Maurier (1834–1896). Caricatures of Oscar Wilde published in *Punch*, 17 July 1880 and 15 January 1881.

George Du Maurier, who joined the staff of *Punch* in 1864, was the late Victorian inheritor of the mantle of W. M. Thackeray. A social satirist, he was equally comfortable working as an artist and as a writer. His great success in literature—the publication in 1894 of the novel *Trilby*—was yet to come. In the 1880s his most important work was certainly his series of cartoons lampooning the Aesthetic movement. Among the recurring characters in these contributions to *Punch* was "Jellaby Postlethwaite," author of *Latter-Day Sapphics*, a poet whose affected airs, swooning postures, and epigrammatic pronouncements were modeled upon the appearance and sayings of Oscar Wilde.

114. Edward Linley Sambourne (1844–1910). Caricature of Oscar Wilde published in *Punch*, 25 June 1881.

Oscar Wilde was one of the favorite targets of the staff of *Punch*, a magazine that remained loyal to the point of view of its middle-class readers and hostile, throughout the 1880s, to the Aesthetes. When Wilde left for New York to begin his lecture tour of America, the *Punch* of 14 January 1882 included a parody interview which began with the "interviewer's" malicious description of Wilde on shipboard:

HIS AESTHETIC APPEARANCE.

He stood, with his large hand passed through his long hair, against a high chimney-piece—which had been painted pea-green, with panels of peacock-blue pottery. . . . He was dressed in a long, snuff-coloured, single-breasted coat, which reached to his heels, and was relieved with a seal-skin collar and cuffs rather the worse for wear. Frayed linen, and an orange silk handkerchief gave a note to the generally artistic coloring of the *ensemble*, while one small daisy drooped despondently in his button-hole. . . . We may state, that the chimney-piece, as well as the seal-skin collar, is the property of OSCAR, and will appear in his Lectures 'On the Growth of Artistic Taste in England.'

The occasion for Edward Linley Sambourne's caricature of Wilde as a gigantic sunflower—a flower emblematic of the Aesthetic movement—was the publication of Wilde's *Poems* (1881).

115. Oscar Wilde. Autograph letter signed to Joseph Marshall Stoddart (1845–1921), [March 1882]. See fig. 15.

In January 1882 Wilde, accompanied by his American publisher J. M. Stoddart, paid a call on Walt Whitman in Camden, New Jersey. This meeting Wilde considered the high point of his American lecture tour, and he lost no time in sending news of Whitman to his friends in England. Among those to whom he wrote was A. C. Swinburne, who had been one of Whitman's earliest English admirers and who had included a poem titled "To Walt Whitman in America" in his *Songs Before Sunrise* (1871).

When Wilde received Swinburne's reply praising Whitman, he transcribed a large portion of it in this letter to Stoddart. Stoddart, in turn, was to pass on the text for publication to his associate in Philadelphia, Robert S. Davis, who was founder of a new Aesthetic American journal called *Our Continent*. In transit from one lecture site to another, Wilde probably wrote the letter in March 1882.

> Somewhere and some time—I
> Dear Mr. Stoddart,   am not sure where or when
>
> I send you the documents but you'd better insert yourself the names of the M.S.S. poems as I do not remember them. I hope to hear soon from you—and to get proof and specimen also. I send you an extract from a letter of Swinburne's which I have just received from him about our grand Walt.
>
> You might care to publish it in the Continent—it runs thus after some personal matter.
>
> XXXXX
>
> I am sincerely interested and gratified by your account of Walt Whitman, and the assurance of his kindly and friendly feeling towards me: and I thank you, no less sincerely, for your kindness in sending me word of it.

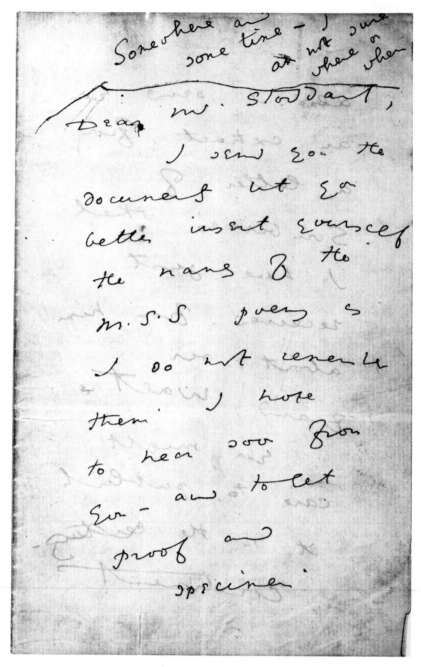

15. Oscar Wilde, first page of autograph letter
signed to J. M. Stoddart [March 1882] (item 115)

As sincerely as I can say, that I shall be freshly obliged to you if you will—should occasion arise—assure him of in my name, that I have by no manner of means relaxed my admiration of his noblest works—such parts, above all, of his writings, as treat of the noblest subjects material and spiritual with which poetry can deal.

I have always thought it, and I believe it will hereafter be generally thought, his highest and surely most enviable distinction distinction [*sic*] is that he never speaks so well as when he speaks of great matters—Liberty, for instance, and Death.

This of course does not imply that I do—rather it implies that I do not—agree with all his theories, or admire all his work in anything like equal measure—a form of admiration which I should by no means desire for myself—and am as little prepared to bestow on another: considering it a form of scarcely indirect insult.

I have not yet received the portrait which should have accompanied your letter: but, as the letter has come safe to hand, no doubt the former will also in due time; for which I do not wait before sending my thanks to Walt Whitman and to yourself.

Yours very truly

A. C. Swinburne

I had intended ten minutes ago to present this to the Continent as a gift, but now after the dreadful bore of copying other peoples long letters and bad handwriting I send it as a contribution—and a very delightful one I think it.

Truly yours
Oscar Wilde

Wilde's initial impulse to make the material a "gift" may have been an acknowledgment of kindness from Stoddart and Davis, who had held receptions for him when he was in Philadelphia (because Wilde's tour had been arranged to publicize American productions of *Patience*, and Stoddart published Gilbert and Sullivan's operas in America, such kindness was not, however, wholly disinterested). Stoddart and Davis were also responsible for the edition of Rennell Rodd's *Rose Leaf and Apple Leaf*, which appeared in 1882 with an introduction by Wilde and an overeffusive dedication to himself.

116. Sir Max Beerbohm. *Rossetti and His Circle*. London, [1922].

In this volume Max Beerbohm included a caricature titled "The Name of Dante Gabriel Rossetti Is Heard for the First Time in the United States of America. Time: 1882. Lecturer: Mr. Oscar Wilde." It was inspired by accounts of Wilde's lecture many years earlier before a group of miners in Leadville, Colorado. In a letter written from Kansas City, Missouri, in April 1882 to one of his London friends, Wilde had described the event:

My audience was entirely miners; their make-up excellent, red shirts and blond beards. . . . I spoke to them of the early Florentines, and they slept as though no crime had ever stained the ravines of their mountain home. I described to them the pictures of Botticelli, and the name, which seemed to them like a new drink, roused them from their dreams, but when I told them . . . of the 'secret of Botticelli' the strong men wept like children . . . and when I quaffed a cocktail without flinching, they unanimously pronounced me . . . 'a bully boy with no glass eye'—artless and spontaneous praise which touched me more than the panegyrics of literary critics ever did or could.

117. William Parrish Chilton (1838–1892). *Columbia: A National Poem.* New York, 1880.

Among the most amusing souvenirs of Oscar Wilde's lecture tour of America was this volume of execrable verse, presented to him by its justly forgotten author, W. P. Chilton. Evidently Chilton believed himself to be following in the path of Walt Whitman in celebrating the national spirit. These lines upon the state of Virginia are typical of the whole:

> *Virginia, first to light the sacred flame!*
> *In her deep woodlands, 'neath a stormy sky,*
> *Roamed wide the pioneers of liberty;*
> *Guardians angelic, hovered o'er the tree*
> *Implanted there, by patriots, pure and free;*
> *Nor ceased to linger, till its umbrage sweet,*
> *Its wide-spread branches, way-worn pilgrims greet.*

118. Ape [Carlo Pellegrini]. *Oscar: Oscar Wilde.* Color lithograph published in *Vanity Fair*, 24 May 1884. (Lent anonymously.) See fig. 16.

As Wilde himself said, "Caricature is the tribute which mediocrity pays to genius."

119. Oscar Wilde. *The Happy Prince and Other Tales.* 1st American ed., 2d impression. Boston, 1890.

Wilde claimed that these works of fantasy, his first published fiction, had their origins in the bedtime stories he told his two small sons. Although their fairy-tale aspects were emphasized by the volume's illustrators, Walter Crane and George Jacomb Hood (1857–1929), these were in fact highly sophisticated works of social criticism, reflecting Wilde's hatred of the middle classes as the enemies of art. The stories were written in a deliberately artificial style; as Wilde explained in a letter, "They are studies in prose, put for Romance's sake into fanciful form: meant . . . for those . . . who find simplicity in a subtle strangeness."

16.   Ape [Carlo Pellegrini], *Oscar: Oscar Wilde,*
color lithograph from *Vanity Fair* (item 118)

This copy of the second American printing is from the library of (William) Clyde Fitch (1865–1909), the American dramatist best known for *Captain Jinks of the Horse Marines* (1901). Fitch, an Aesthete himself, was one of Wilde's most ardent admirers; the two met, probably in 1890, and Fitch was given a presentation copy of the English edition of this book. Pasted into this copy, along with a short autograph note from Wilde to Fitch, is a photograph of Wilde's wife, Constance, with their elder son Cyril—from both of whom Wilde would be separated forever after 1895, when he was convicted and imprisoned on charges of homosexuality.

120. Constance Lloyd Wilde (1857–1898). *There Was Once.* 1st American ed. New York, 1888.

Despite his professed loathing for the middle classes, Wilde never completely escaped his need for their approval and even love. When he married in 1884, he chose as his bride a sheltered and conventional young woman whom he began by idealizing as a "grave, slight violet-eyed little Artemis." As a couple, however, they would soon prove an utter mismatch. She disliked publicity, felt uncomfortable in the fast circles in which Wilde traveled, and resented his intimate attachments to other men, the true nature of which were a mystery to her. The only bond between husband and wife was their shared love of children.

This rare venture into print by Mrs. Oscar Wilde is, appropriately enough, a book for young readers.

121. Oscar Wilde. *The Picture of Dorian Gray,* in *Lippincott's Monthly Magazine.* Philadelphia and London, July 1890.

Wilde's enduring tale of a man whose portrait becomes the mirror of his soul aroused the ire of both English and American critics on its publication. The chief objections were to its cynicism and apparent absence of moral purpose. Typical of the reactions was this comment by an anonymous reviewer for the *Daily Chronicle:* "It is a tale spawned from the leprous literature of the French *Décadents*—a poisonous book, the atmosphere of which is heavy with the mephitic odours of moral and spiritual putrefaction . . . which might be horrible and fascinating but for its . . . flippant philosophisings, and the contaminating trail of garish vulgarity which is over all Mr. Wilde's elaborate Wardour Street aestheticism and obtrusively cheap scholarship." For the publication of the novel in book form in 1891, Wilde expanded the original thirteen chapters to nineteen and considerably revised the whole, retaining, however, all its objectionable matter.

122. Oscar Wilde. *Salomé: Drame en un acte.* Paris and London, 1893.

This, the true first edition of Wilde's famous play—published a year before the English version with Aubrey Beardsley's illustrations—is inscribed by Wilde to Florence Stoker and accompanied by a letter to her postmarked 21 February 1893. Wilde wrote, "Will you accept a copy of *Salome*—my strange venture in a tongue that is not my own, but that I love as one loves an instrument of music on which one has not played before." Florence Balcombe (1858–1937), known to Wilde in his youth as "Florrie," was an old friend from Dublin. In 1878 she had married Bram Stoker (1847–1912), the future author of *Dracula* (1897).

123. Sir Max Beerbohm. *The Works of Max Beerbohm.* London and New York, 1896.

This volume—which, although facetiously titled *The Works*, was in fact Max Beerbohm's first book—contains the essay "1880," a prematurely retrospective examination in 1894 of a "period . . . now so remote from us that much in it is nearly impossible to understand . . . left in the mists of antiquity that involve it." Assuming the pose of an enthusiastic historian reanimating the past, Beerbohm exhumed in the essay such figures as "Mr. Oscar Wilde . . . [to whom] was due no small part of the social vogue that Beauty began to enjoy. Fired by his fervid words, men and women hurled their mahogany into the streets. . . . Dados arose upon every wall, sunflowers and the feathers of peacocks curved in every corner."

This copy is the first English edition, inscribed to the author's nephew by marriage, Alan Parsons (1887–1933), the civil servant and drama critic.

 James McNeill Whistler

124. James McNeill Whistler (1834–1903). *Self-portrait.* Etching and drypoint, 1871. (Lent by University of Virginia Art Museum)

This self-portrait shows the influence of Rembrandt, whose work James McNeill Whistler had studied in Holland in the 1850s.

125. Spy [Sir Leslie Ward]. *A Symphony: James McNeill Whistler.* Color lithograph published in *Vanity Fair,* 12 January 1878. (Lent by Cecil Y. Lang)

Whistler, in his pose of the dandy, is seen here at the height of his notoriety—between the time of John Ruskin's attack upon him in *Fors Clavigera* (1877) and the opening in November 1878 of the trial of his libel suit against Ruskin.

126. James McNeill Whistler. *Mr. Whistler's "Ten O'Clock."* 1st published ed. London, 1888. (Lent anonymously)

On 20 February 1885 Whistler gave a lecture on matters of art at
Princes Hall in London. His talk, repeated at Cambridge and
Oxford, became known as the "Ten O'Clock," after its unlikely hour
of delivery. Although it was poorly received, even by Whistler's
friends Swinburne and Wilde, it had a profound effect upon later
Aesthetic theory. Calling himself "The Preacher," Whistler began
his lecture by presenting an almost religious view of art as a "god-
dess" who was "selfishly occupied with her own perfection only—
having no desire to teach—seeking and finding the beautiful in all
conditions." This defense of art for art's sake was coupled with an
attack upon historicism and upon the notion of art as having educational and moral value—concepts universally accepted by the Victorian public in general and by readers of Ruskin in particular. Even
more radical, however, was Whistler's vision of the artist as an
outsider, a member of an elite class, who aimed not to copy nature but
to surpass it.

Although the lecture was privately printed in 1885, this is the first
published edition, designed by the author himself and issued by
Chatto and Windus in 1888. This copy belonged to the designer and
critic Lewis F. Day (1845–1910), an associate of William Morris.
Day embellished his signature around Whistler's butterfly mono-
gram on the front cover.

127. James McNeill Whistler. *Nocturne.* Lithotint, 1878. (Lent by University of Virginia Art Museum)

This print was made just before the start of the *Whistler* v. *Ruskin*
trial and represents the very aspect of Whistler's art to which the
latter had objected, i.e., its nebulosity and lack of narrative content.
The scene is Battersea, then as now an industrial area of London on
the south side of the Thames; its mood is captured in a passage in
Whistler's "Ten O'Clock" lecture in which he describes the moment
each day "when the evening mist clothes the riverside with poetry, as
with a veil, and the poor buildings lose themselves in the dim sky,
and the tall chimneys become campanili, and the warehouses are
palaces in the night, and the whole city hangs in the heavens."

128. George Du Maurier. *Distinguished Amateurs: The Art-Critic.* Pen
and ink drawing, 1880. (Lent by William B. O'Neal)

Oscar Wilde was not the sole target of George Du Maurier's anti-
Aesthetic satires of the 1880s; Whistler also shared that distinction.
In Du Maurier's stable of pretentious types was a fictitious painter
named Maudle, who "although unsuccessful as an Exhibitor" was

rapidly "getting known to Fame through the exertions of his Literary Friends," much as was Whistler himself. Maudle often traveled in the company of his equally imaginary admirer, the poet Jellaby Postlethwaite (based largely on Wilde), whom he had painted as "Dead Narcissus." In this cartoon which appeared in *Punch* in 1880, another member of the Aesthetes' circle, the critic Prigsby (an invention who may have been inspired by Walter Pater) was made to reveal unwittingly his own ignorance of art:

Prigsby (contemplating his friend Maudle's last Picture). 'THE HEAD OF ALEXIS IS DISTINCTLY DIVINE! NOR CAN *I*, IN THE WHOLE RANGE OF ANCIENT, MEDIAEVAL, OR MODERN ART, RECALL ANYTHING QUITE SO FAIR AND PRECIOUS: UNLESS IT BE, PERHAPS, THE HEAD OF THAT SUPREMEST MASTERPIECE OF GREEK SCULPTCHAH, THE ILYSSUS, WHEREOF INDEED, IN A CERTAIN GRACIOUS MODELLING OF THE LOVELY NECK, AND IN THE SUBTLY DELECTABLE CURVES OF THE CHEEK AND CHIN, IT FAINTLY, YET MOST EXQUISITELY, REMINDS ME!'

Chorus of Fair Enthusiasts (who still believe in Prigsby). 'OH, YES—YES!—OF COURSE!—THE ILYSSUS!!—IN THE ELGIN MARBLES, YOU KNOW!!! *HOW TRUE!!!!*'

ALWAYS READY TO LEARN, AND DEEPLY IMPRESSED BY THE EXTENT OF PRIGSBY'S INFORMATION, OUR GALLANT FRIEND THE COLONEL TAKES AN EARLY OPPORTUNITY OF VISITING THE BRITISH MUSEUM, IN ORDER TO STUDY THE HEAD AND NECK OF

THE ILYSSUS!

As was clear from Du Maurier's illustration, the joke is that the Ilyssus has, of course, neither head nor neck.

129. James McNeill Whistler. *Count Robert de Montesquiou.* Lithograph, 1894–95. (Lent by University of Virginia Art Museum)

Count Robert de Montesquiou (1855–1921), poet and aristocrat, was the leading French Aesthete of his day. He was one of the models for J. K. Huysman's hero Des Esseintes in *A Rebours* (1884), a novel which, in turn, had a marked influence upon Oscar Wilde's *The Picture of Dorian Gray.* Introduced possibly by Henry James, Whistler met Montesquiou in 1884, and their friendship culminated in the painting *Arrangement in Black and Gold,* Whistler's large portrait of the count (now in the Frick Collection, New York). It is thought that Whistler made this lithograph because he disliked a photogravure that had been done of the *Arrangement.*

130. James McNeill Whistler. *The Gentle Art of Making Enemies.* London, 1890.

Dedicated to "the rare Few, who, early in Life, have rid Themselves of the Friendship of the Many," *The Gentle Art of Making Enemies* was Whistler's artistic manifesto: a combination of imaginatively recast "facts" about his life, history of his progress in the art world, and responses to the attacks he had suffered from old-guard critics. In it he collected and rewrote his earlier pamphlets, *Whistler vs. Ruskin* (1878) and *Mr. Whistler's "Ten O'Clock,"* adding to them excerpts from articles and letters, together with his own acerbic comments. *The Gentle Art of Making Enemies* was also the high point of Whistler's work in book design. In its asymmetrical typography and economical use of ornament, the volume is like no other connected with the Aesthetic movement. So perfectly are the text and design matched that Max Beerbohm could write in 1903, "Read any page . . . and you will hear a voice in it, and see a face in it, and see gestures in it. And none of these is quite like any known to you. It matters not that you never knew Whistler. . . . You see him and know him here. . . . He projected through printed words the clean-cut image and clear-ringing echo of himself."

131. Sir William Nicholson (1872–1949). *James McNeill Whistler.* Color lithograph, 1897.

William Nicholson, better known now as the illustrator of Margery Williams Bianco's *The Velveteen Rabbit* (1922), was one of the many younger artists of the 1880s and 1890s to be influenced strongly by Whistler's work. This portrait of Whistler was prompted by Whistler's compliments to Nicholson upon the latter's famous woodcut portrait of Queen Victoria. It was issued by Heinemann, Whistler's publisher, in a series that also included portraits of Sarah Bernhardt and Rudyard Kipling.

Framed with it is a short autograph note from Whistler, probably dating from about 1885 and dealing with a "paragraph" about him printed in a London newspaper.

❧ THE NEW FICTION ❧

 *George Meredith* ❧

132. Sir Max Beerbohm. *Our First Novelist: George Meredith*. Color lithograph published in *Vanity Fair*, 24 September 1896. (Lent by Cecil Y. Lang)

The caricature is a particularly affectionate one, for Max Beerbohm, as David Cecil noted in *Max: A Biography* (1964), considered George Meredith "the greatest author alive and possibly the greatest English author since Shakespeare."

133. George Meredith (1828–1909). *Emilia in England*. 3 vols. London, 1864.

Emilia in England, George Meredith's story of a "feminine musical genius," was published at the author's own expense after he became worried about "what the British P[ublic]." would "say to a Finis that holds aloft no nuptial torch" (in other words, that did not end in the heroine's marriage). The book was not reprinted in England until 1886, when its title was changed to *Sandra Belloni*. It had, however, been translated into French almost immediately upon publication in 1864. This copy may be the one from which the French version was done, for it is inscribed to the translator by Meredith on the title page, "Monsieur E. D. Forgues—Hommages de l'Auteur." Later it belonged to Arthur Symons, who purchased it from a Paris bookstall in 1889.

134. George Meredith. Autograph letter signed to Charles Lewis Hind (1862–1927), 11 November 1900.

In this letter to the editor of the *Academy*, Meredith wrote, "The fact that working men & women can take an interest in my work seems an assurance that I have dealt with life, & is more to me than reviewers' eulogy." Laudable though Meredith's expression of democratic impulses may be, it is hard to imagine how the working classes in general would have responded to his prose style—a complex and knotty one that could only be disentangled by the erudite.

135. George Meredith. *Diana of the Crossways: A Novel.* 3 vols. London, 1885.

George Meredith was among the few male authors of his generation to be actively sympathetic to the cause of feminism (or "womanism," as it was often called before the 1890s). His method of lending support to the advancement of women's rights was not to write pro-suffrage pamphlets or speeches but to populate his novels with heroines who were in themselves arguments in favor of equality: independent and resourceful women of wit, intelligence, and creativity bravely facing the restrictions of a narrow-minded society. Looking back upon his earlier life, Meredith classed himself among the formerly narrow-minded. The blame he took upon himself for the failure of his first marriage and for the premature death of his wife had much to do with his championship of fictional creations such as Diana, the rebellious protagonist of this novel. The heroine of *Diana of the Crossways*, which appeared serially in a shorter version in the *Fortnightly Review* (1884), was commonly believed to have been modeled upon the poet Caroline Sheridan Norton (Lady Stirling-Maxwell), who died in 1877.

136. George Gissing (1857–1903). Autograph letter signed to his brother, Algernon Gissing (1860–1937), 29 April 1885.

Even before Meredith, in his capacity as publisher's reader for Chapman and Hall, helped George Gissing in 1884 with revisions of the manuscript of *The Unclassed*, Gissing had been a worshipful admirer of the elder novelist. He wrote to his brother (soon to be a fellow novelist): "By hook or by crook get hold of 'Diana of the Crossways'. . . . The book is right glorious—Shakespeare in modern English; but, mind you, to be read twice, or, if need be, thrice. There is a preface, which is a plea for philosophic fiction; an admirable piece of writing, the English alone rendering it worthy of the carefullest pondering. More 'brain stuff' in the book than in any I have read for long."

137. Arthur Symons (1865–1945). *An Introduction to the Study of Browning.* London, 1886.

A young Welshman with no advanced education, Arthur Symons began his career by writing an introduction to one of the publications of the New Shakespeare Society. This put him in contact with the society's founder, F. J. Furnivall, who introduced him to members of the London literary establishment. *An Introduction to the Study of Browning,* Symons's first book, was "written as an act of homage to the poet worshipped from boyhood"; it was dedicated to another of the author's heroes, George Meredith. Symons wrote that the book's publication brought him several rewards: "the generous praise of Walter Pater in the *Guardian,* which led to the beginning of my friendship with him; then . . . a single sentence from George Meredith: 'you have done knightly service to a brave leader'; lastly . . . a letter from Browning himself, in which he said 'How can I manage to thank—much more praise—what, in its generosity of appreciation, makes the poorest recognition 'come too near the praising of myself.'"

138. Arthur Symons. *Days and Nights.* London, 1889. (Lent by Franklin Gilliam Rare Books)

   The epigraph to Symons's *Days and Nights* was drawn from George Meredith's *Modern Love,* and at least one poem, a sonnet sequence called "A Lover's Progress," showed homage in style and content to Meredith. The book was, however, dedicated in "all gratitude and admiration" to Walter Pater; as produced by the firm of Macmillan, Pater's own publishers, it even resembled closely the latter's works in its physical design. In the poem "Prologue," Symons echoed Pater's melancholy view of life as fleeting and bitter, enriched only by moments of passion or beauty, as he defined the nature of Art:

> *The winter of the world is in her soul,*
> *The pity of the little lives we lead,*
> *And the long slumber and the certain goal,*
> *And after us our own rebellious seed.*

> *Therefore the notes are blended in her breath,*
> *And nights and days one equal song unites;*
> *Yet, since of man with trouble born to death*
> *She sings, her song is less of Days than Nights.*

   George Gissing

139. Sir William Rothenstein (1872–1945). *George Gissing.* Lithograph, 1897. (Lent anonymously)

   This lithograph, published in William Rothenstein's *English Portraits* in 1898, is the only known depiction of George Gissing by an artist. In his autobiography *Men and Memories* (1931), Rothenstein wrote of Gissing:

I liked him very much—a wistful, sensitive nature, a little saddened
I thought, and perhaps a little lacking in vitality, but with a tender
sense of beauty. He had just come back from Italy . . . but had
met with unexpected sorrow at home, on hearing that one of his
friends . . . had recently come to a tragic end. A man of rare culture,
he said of his friend, with strong puritanical inhibitions; yet he had
certain inclinations against which he had struggled in vain all his life.
On account of these, and feeling he could fight them no longer, he had
suddenly shot himself. Gissing, much more than Hardy, seemed
obsessed by the melancholy side of life.

140. George Gissing. Autograph letter signed to his brother, Algernon,
27 December 1882.

Here Gissing described the aftermath of his separation from his
first wife:

17 Oakley Crescent S.W.

My dear Alg.,   Dec. 27th 1882.

Close upon the astonishing intelligence conveyed in my last, I have
to send you news of changes. My wife, in brief, has gone to live with
some people in Brixton, taking for her own use one half of the
furniture, & leaving me the rest. I had proposed at first (in view of
the serious diminution of income consequent upon cessation of Rus-
sian article) to take one little bedroom for myself somewhere in this
neighbourhood. Mrs. Coward stepped in as my saviour by proposing
that I should have a little back room of their own, & so save all the
fearful trouble of removal, etc. Accordingly, here I am in my new
room: very, very small & chock full of things, but redolent of quiet
work. My rent will be 7/– weekly, including all attendance! By
midsummer, I hope to have another novel finished. For a bed, I use
my sofa (there would not be room for a proper bed,) hiding away all
the clothing during the day-time. My washing apparatus disappears
in a convenient little cupboard. I am once more quiet in mind. My
wife receives £1 weekly; so that my expenses are still heavy enough.

With the Giffards I compromised matters by asking for a guinea &
a half a week, & received it.

Something tells me that a new period has opened. I enclose a note
[Frederic] Harrison has sent me. Maybe the last sentence is true.
Bentleys are men of standing, & there is every hope of their making a
success of this book, in which case they will be glad to get another—
but by no means on the same terms.

Affectionately,
GRG.

I have decided (as I told you) to omit the *R* in my authorial signature.

Bentleys, the publishers, had accepted the manuscript of *Mrs. Grundy's Enemies*, which Smith, Elder had rejected as too radical and "painful" for the subscribers to circulating libraries. While the book was in the proof stage, the publishers objected to certain scenes and dialogues as overexplicit. Gissing worked until 1884 upon revisions, but the book was never issued. The manuscript and proofs were subsequently lost.

141. George Gissing. *Demos: A Story of English Socialism.* 3 vols. London, 1886.

In the course of telling this melodramatic story of a working-class man who inherits and loses a fortune, Gissing wished to give a picture of the political turmoil of the 1880s—especially of the growing power of the lower classes, whom he feared and disliked. In the cause of truth to life, he attended a meeting of the Socialist League, formed in 1885 with William Morris as one of its leaders (Gissing allegedly modeled the fictional character named Westlake on Morris). Despite the many descriptions of radical speeches and riots, the novel comes alive only in its scenes of domestic conflict. In these battles between a brutal workingman and his idealistic, educated wife, one can find reflections—albeit with sexes and social positions reversed—of the violent quarrels between Gissing and his first wife, "Nell" Harrison Gissing, a former prostitute.

142. George Gissing. *The Nether World: A Novel.* 3 vols. London, 1889.

Gissing's dread of the consequences of Social Darwinism—a philosophy that encouraged the competitive spirit and reserved admiration for the "fittest" alone—led him in 1882 to write "The Hope of Pessimism," an essay advocating charity toward and compassion for all mankind. Although Gissing chose not to publish this essay, he drew heavily upon it while writing many of his novels of the 1880s. Michael Snowdon, a character in *The Nether World*, became the spokesman for the very position Gissing himself had taken:

> If only we had pity on one another, all the worst things we suffer from in this world would be at an end. It's because men's hearts are hard that life is so full of misery. If we could only learn to be kind and gentle and forgiving—never mind anything else. We act as if we were all each other's enemies; we can't be merciful, because we expect no mercy; we struggle to get as much as we can for ourselves and care nothing for others. Think about it; never let it go out of your mind.

Ironically, Snowdon's inability to sympathize with the particular weaknesses of those around him, despite his theory, results in the failure of his plans for social reform. The novel, which in its methods and materials owes much to Naturalism, ends in a mood of defeat.

143. George Gissing. *The Emancipated: A Novel.* 3 vols. London, 1890.

In *The Emancipated*, Gissing displayed his increasing sympathy with two of the advanced causes of the 1880s: Aestheticism and feminism. The writing of the novel followed a trip to France and Italy, during which he recorded in his diary on 19 October 1888 his loss of interest in the fate of "the people" and his shift toward an elitist position: "On crossing the Channel I have become a poet pure and simple, or perhaps it would be better to say an idealist student of art." The hero of his novel is also an elitist, a painter with no desire to offer the public a moral message: "The one object I have in life is to paint a bit of the world just as I see it," he announces. This artist becomes involved with a group of women, several of whom are consciously struggling to break free of conventional roles—to become emancipated. Although Gissing's ambivalence toward their cause is evident, the light in which he depicts them as individuals is surprisingly kind.

144. George Gissing. *New Grub Street: A Novel.* 3 vols. London, 1891. (Lent anonymously)

Gissing's most celebrated novel was one of the first works of fiction in England to center wholly upon the subject of writing itself, and in particular on the creative and commercial obstacles faced by professional authors of the 1880s, a time in which formats of publication and audience tastes were changing with great rapidity. Into the pathetic tale of a novelist whose ideals will not allow him to compromise with the demands of Philistine publishers, and whose inspiration is too scanty to enable him to make a living from "Art" alone, Gissing poured the facts of his own unfortunate career in the 1880s. He showed, moreover, his sympathy with the ultrarealist aesthetic of the followers of French Naturalism in the portrait of another writer, a minor character named Biffen, who kills himself after the public rejects his chef d'oeuvre, the documentary novel *Mr. Bailey, Grocer.*

 *Thomas Hardy*

145. Spy [Sir Leslie Ward]. *Tess: Thomas Hardy.* Color lithograph published in *Vanity Fair*, 4 June 1892. (Lent by Cecil Y. Lang)

146. Thomas Hardy (1840–1928). *The Trumpet-Major: A Tale.* 3 vols. London, 1880.

Thomas Hardy's historical tale, involving rustics during the Napoleonic Wars, was like all of his novels of the 1880s published first in periodical form (in this case, in *Good Words*, January to December 1880) before being revised for issue as a book. Somewhat atypical of the author's fiction of the period, *The Trumpet-Major* represented in part Hardy's effort to write the sort of comic and romantic work that would please magazine editors, to whom he promoted the manuscript as "a cheerful story, without views or opinions, & [that] is intended to wind up happily."

147. Donald Macleod (1831–1911). Autograph letter signed to Richard Dodderidge Blackmore (1825–1900), 4 February 1880.

Donald Macleod, the editor of *Good Words*, wrote to R. D. Blackmore, author of *Lorna Doone* (1869), who was also a contributor to the magazine, about the serialization of Hardy's novel: "I think Mr. Hardy's Trumpet-Major is going to turn out very successful— and so also is Jean Ingelow's clever story. I have seen only the first six parts of Hardy's but it is very graphic."

148. Thomas Hardy. *A Laodicean: or, The Castle of the De Stancys. A Story of To-Day.* 3 vols. London, 1881.

Although subtitled *A Story of To-Day*, Hardy's novel had more to do with the clash between today and yesterday, symbolized by the fate of a medieval castle under restoration by its new owner, the daughter of a railway magnate. Hardy's own ambivalence toward the notion of progress and inability to rest content with "To-Day" is summed up early in the novel, as the hero, a young architect named Somerset, first surveys the castle and notices that a telegraph has been installed in it:

> There was a certain unexpectedness in the fact that the hoary memorial of a stolid antagonism to the interchange of ideas, the monument of hard distinctions in blood and race, of deadly mistrust of one's neighbour in spite of the Church's teaching, and of a sublime unconsciousness of any other force than a brute one, should be the goal of a machine which beyond everything may be said to symbolize cosmopolitan views and the intellectual and moral kinship of all mankind. In that light the little buzzing wire had a far finer significance to the student Somerset than the vast walls which neighboured it. But the modern fever and fret which consumes people before they can grow old was also signified by the wire; and this aspect of to-day did not contrast well with the fairer side of feudalism—leisure, light-hearted generosity, intense friendships, hawks, hounds, revels, healthy complexions, freedom from care, and such a living power in architectural art as the world may never again see.

Called by the *Saturday Review* a new departure in the wrong direction, the novel, which was written for serial publication in *Harper's Magazine* and completed while Hardy was suffering from a serious illness, was never among the author's most popular. This copy is the first English edition. Harper and Brothers of New York had issued the book slightly earlier as a volume in their Franklin Square Library.

149. Thomas Hardy. *Two on a Tower: A Romance.* 3 vols. London, 1882.

In a notebook entry for July 1881, Hardy observed: "The real, if unavowed, purpose of fiction is to give pleasure by gratifying the love of the uncommon in human experience, mental or corporeal. . . . The writer's problem is, how to strike the balance between the uncommon and the ordinary so as on the one hand to give interest, on the other to give reality." For Hardy, one solution to the problem was to draw the "uncommon" from the realm of science. The tower of the title is the makeshift observatory frequented by the hero, whose studies have taught him that "for all the wonder of these everlasting stars, eternal spheres, and what not, they are not everlasting, they are not eternal; they burn out like candles" and who asks, therefore, whether "those who exert their imaginative powers to bury themselves in the depths of that universe merely strain their faculties to gain a new horror?" In this story of the astronomer's romance with an ill-fated noblewoman, Hardy wished, as he announced in his preface to the novel, "to set the emotional history of two infinitesimal lives against the stupendous background of the stellar universe." The public in general treated his attempt with incomprehension—the reviewer for the *Spectator*, for instance, complaining, "There is not a single gleam of probability in the plot, and what good end can be served by violating all natural motives in order to produce such unpleasant results?"

Before its publication in book form, *Two on a Tower* appeared as a serial in the *Atlantic Monthly.*

150. Thomas Hardy. Autograph letter signed to an unidentified editor, 16 December 1882.

This letter may have been addressed to Alfred Austin (1835–1913), the future poet laureate, who was the first editor of the *National Review*, a magazine begun in March 1883. Hardy wrote:

Dear Sir,

I have nothing ready for a magazine at present, beyond what has been arranged for. If you will let me know more particulars of the magazine, when the project is further advanced, I will give the subject my best consideration.

151. Thomas Hardy. *The Woodlanders*. 3 vols. London, 1887.

Hardy began work on this novel while completing another "Wessex" tale, *The Mayor of Casterbridge* (1886). *The Woodlanders* remained among his personal favorites, a preference not shared by most critics on its appearance. The objections that they raised were, as usual, on grounds of faulty morality; as the critic for the *London Quarterly and Holborn Review* noted sadly, "[t]he description of the Dorset peasantry, as to their character and manners, and the painting of the local scenery, may be perfect; but the moral of the story is very bad." Hardy, however, rejected the role into which he was being cast by such critics and demanded instead the right to "paint" a picture of life as he saw it, without concern for the effect such unpleasant truth might have on the unsophisticated. In "The Profitable Reading of Fiction," an essay published in the *Forum* of March 1888, he would defend his position: "A novel which does moral injury to a dozen imbeciles, and has bracing results upon a thousand intellects of normal vigor, can justify its existence; and probably a novel was never written by the purest-minded author for which there could not be found some moral invalid or other whom it was capable of harming." The first edition of *The Woodlanders* in book form followed its appearance as a serial in *Macmillan's Magazine*.

152. Thomas Hardy. *Tess of the D'Urbervilles: A Pure Woman Faithfully Presented*. 3 vols. London, [1891].

Early acquaintance with the evolutionary theories of Darwin and Huxley seemed to produce in Hardy an extreme pessimism as to the course of human civilization and nature, both of which he saw as in decay. Given his belief in the inevitability of such decline, it was impossible for him to accept conventional moral teachings, which emphasized the responsibility of the individual for his or her own actions and fate. Hardy's charitable attitude toward the sexually experienced heroine of this novel—an opinion reflected in the subtitle, *A Pure Woman*—was not, however, shared by his middle-class readers. He began work on the novel in 1888. The uncompleted manuscript was turned down in 1889 by the first two periodicals, *Murray's Magazine* and *Macmillan's Magazine*, to which it was sent as a serial. When it finally appeared in the *Graphic* (July to December, 1891), two sections were missing, rejected by a cautious editor. These had been published earlier, as separate stories, in more ad-

vanced periodicals, Frank Harris's *Fortnightly Review* and W. E.
Henley's *National Observer*.

 Emile Zola and George Moore

153. T [Theobald Chartran (1849–1907)]. *French Realism: Emile Zola.*
Color lithograph published in *Vanity Fair*, 24 January 1880. (Lent by
Cecil Y. Lang)

154. Emile Zola (1840–1902). *Mes Haines.* New ed. Paris, 1879.
　　To the later Victorians, Emile Zola was the touchstone by which
they measured how advanced were their own views. For many, Zola
represented the "sewer" of French Naturalism from which a morally
repugnant stench was wafting over to England. This olfactory metaphor was so pervasive that it found its way even into the criticism of
the otherwise tolerant and sophisticated American Henry James.
Reviewing *Nana* for the *Parisian* of 26 February 1880, James wrote:
"M. Zola's uncleanness is not a thing to linger upon, but it is a thing
to speak of. . . . *Nana* has little to envy its predecessors. The book
is, perhaps, not pervaded by that ferociously bad smell which blows
through *L'Assommoir* like an emanation from an open drain and
makes the perusal of the history of Gervaise and Coupeau very much
such an ordeal as a crossing of the Channel in a November gale;
but . . . *Nana* is, in all conscience, untidy enough." In the same
review, however, James showed that he had been able to overcome his
dislike of the results and to sympathize with the intentions behind the
composition of the novel. His account of the philosophy of Naturalism—gleaned not only from Zola's fiction but from works such as
this volume of critical essays—is indeed remarkably just.
　　The copy displayed belonged to Henry James.

155. Emile Zola. *Nana: A Realistic Novel.* 1st English ed. Translated
without abridgment from the 127th French ed. London, 1884.
　　The introduction to England of Zola's novels—especially of
Nana, the life history of an amoral and unrepentant Parisian prostitute—was considered by many readers (and even by Parliament,
which debated the "Zola question" on 8 May 1888) a symbolic act of
effrontery against conventional moral standards, to be stopped in its
tracks before the insult spread. The obvious target for the National
Vigilance Association, which was formed to protect the public from
such outrages to decency, was the publisher responsible for issuing
the translations of Zola's works in England, Henry Vizetelly (1820–

1894). In 1888, at the instigation of the association, Vizetelly was tried and convicted on charges of obscenity and fined £100 for publishing the English edition of *La Terre*. One year later, after continuing to distribute what the association called "pernicious" literature, Vizetelly was rearrested and, although he was nearly seventy years of age, sent to prison for three months.

The decorated vignette on the front cover of *Nana* shows, in the figure of the Aesthetic gentleman, what may be a caricature of Oscar Wilde inspired by the *Punch* cartoons of George Du Maurier.

156. George Moore (1852–1933). *Confessions of a Young Man*. London, 1888. See fig. 17.

When asked whether he knew George Moore, Oscar Wilde was said to have replied, "Know him? I know him so well that I haven't spoken to him in ten years." No one, however, really knew Moore, an Irishman whose penchant for exaggerating his own accomplishments (especially his amorous ones) and for altering the facts of his past made him notorious. His interest in himself went beyond mere egotism to achieve the status of artistic preoccupation. Between 1887 and 1926 he produced seven different versions of the *Confessions* alone—to say nothing of several unrelated volumes of autobiography—for English, American, and French editions, each one involving considerable revision of style and content. The first of these was the shortest, a version in nine chapters that appeared serially from July through November 1887 in *Time, a Monthly Magazine*. The first edition in book form, published in 1888, comprised twelve chapters.

In 1870, on coming into his inheritance, Moore had left Ireland "for Paris and Art," to study painting with the Impressionists and to learn fiction-writing from the Naturalists. Moore was among the earliest English-speaking apostles of the new movements in France; after settling in London in 1879, he became one of the first spokesmen for and promoters of the aesthetics of Manet, Degas, the Goncourt brothers, and Zola. The *Confessions*, as well as revealing the author's fascination with himself, also conveyed nicely the fascination and excitement that young Aesthetes of Moore's generation felt in the presence of French culture, which represented for them the liberation from English Philistinism.

This copy was inscribed and presented by the author to Lady Derby. The cover design is by the French artist Jacques-Emile Blanche (1862–1942); the frontispiece portrait is an early etching by William Strang (1859–1921).

17.   George Moore, *Confessions of a Young Man*
(London, 1888), front cover design by Jacques-Emile
Blanche (item 156)

157. George Moore. *Literature at Nurse: or Circulating Morals*. London, 1885. (Lent anonymously)

Although they were destined to lose their power in the 1890s, largely due to the efforts of rebels such as Moore, the major circulating libraries (especially Mudie's and Smith's) exerted a stranglehold upon fiction in the 1880s. As George Gissing would show in *New Grub Street*, they were able to impose upon helpless writers their preferences as to both form and content, prescribing three-volume or triple-decker novels that contained no hint of immorality. When, however, Mudie's banned from its shelves his novel *A Mummer's Wife* (1885), a realistic tale of infidelity and alcoholism among the lower classes, Moore countered by issuing this pamphlet. His method of argument was unusual; he demonstrated, through excerpts and plot summaries, that three popular novels to be found on Mudie's current Select Library list were far more obscene and pernicious than his work, which was merely a faithful depiction of reality.

158. George Moore. *A Mere Accident*. London, 1887.

Naturalism was, in part, the response of literature to the new discoveries of science, especially to the theories of Darwin and his followers. Seeing the individual as nothing more than a member of a species and as subject, like all other organisms, to the determining influences of biological inheritance and environmental pressures, the Naturalist writer attempted to study his or her characters with the same objectivity and to expose their inner workings with the same thoroughness as a scientist would employ in dissecting a specimen. In the 1880s George Moore produced a series of fictional studies, two of them bearing the same subtitle (*A Realistic Novel*) as a warning to squeamish readers. Among the works of his realistic phase was this examination of the psychological state of a young Catholic Aesthete (said to have been based on the Irish patriot Edward Martyn), which was published by Henry Vizetelly, who was also Zola's publisher in England. Moore later revised *A Mere Accident* and renamed it *John Norton;* it became one of the three novellas he collected under the title *Celibates* in 1895.

159. Sic [Walter Sickert (1860–1942)]. *Esther Waters: George Moore.* Color lithograph published in *Vanity Fair,* 21 January 1897. (Lent by Cecil Y. Lang)

Walter Sickert, one of Whistler's many followers, was an early English exponent of the new French art. He was also a member of the group that exhibited in 1889 as the London Impressionists and issued a catalogue which echoed Whistler's "Ten O'Clock" in form and content. Moore met Sickert in the early 1880s and wrote of him in an essay about the New English Art Club, an organization with which both men were allied. The essay was collected in *Modern Painting* (1893). This caricature, one of only three done by Sickert for *Vanity Fair*, is far less kind to Moore than was his oil portrait reproduced in the *Yellow Book* in 1895 and now in the Tate Gallery, London.

160. George Moore. *Esther Waters*. 2d ed. London, 1899.

The seeds of Moore's huge popular and critical success of 1894, the novel *Esther Waters*, were actually planted in his Zola period of the 1880s. Although Moore would eventually repudiate Naturalism as a bankrupt aesthetic, his study of the English netherworld through the eyes of a fallen servant girl still showed the marks of his indebtedness to his French masters. In the course of narrating the sympathetic title character's doomed attempts at building a respectable life for herself and her illegitimate child, Moore exposed the villainies of the double standards of British justice and social morality, which enforced one law for the rich, another for the poor.

This copy is the second edition, inscribed and presented by the author to Lady Dorothy Nevill (1826–1913), a minor author who was, as Moore wrote here, "a friend of many years."

ROMANCE WRITERS

Robert Louis Stevenson

161. Two photographs of Robert Louis Stevenson (1850–1894). Silver prints, ca. 1885. See fig. 18.

These studio portraits, which capture Robert Louis Stevenson's swaggering, Bohemian air, seem to date from the same year as John Singer Sargent's controversial painting of the writer; indeed, they show Stevenson wearing the identical lounging costume. Although shown in these photographs casually smoking a cigarette, Stevenson suffered all his life from tuberculosis and, despite a last attempt at recovering his health by settling in Samoa in 1889, died at the age of forty-four after years of debilitating illness.

162. Robert Louis Stevenson. *Familiar Studies of Men and Books*. London, 1882.

Stevenson called this, his second collection of essays, the "readings of a literary vagrant." It might better be termed the marriage of the Scots and Aesthetic aspects of his literary interests, its contents being as varied as "Some Aspects of Robert Burns," "Walt Whitman," "François Villon," and "John Knox and Women." The book's decorated covers are, however, decidedly Aesthetic—*japonisme* filtered through the eye of a commercial Victorian publisher.

163. Robert Louis Stevenson. *A Child's Garden of Verses*. London, 1885.

Stevenson began writing poems supposedly "for children" in 1881. Two years later he collected what he had composed in a privately printed pamphlet titled *Penny Whistles*. With some revisions and additions this was published in 1885 as the now famous *A Child's Garden of Verses*. Although couched in the form of rhymes for

18. Contemporary photograph of Robert Louis
Stevenson (item 161)

the nursery these were, nonetheless, stylistically sophisticated poems that showed the influence of his studies of Scottish folk ballads.

164. Robert Louis Stevenson. *Kidnapped: Being Memoirs of the Adventures of David Balfour in the Year 1751.* . . . London, 1886.

In the early 1880s Stevenson's reputation was that of a minor man of letters. By 1882 he had published six books, not one of them a best-seller. Recently married and in poor health, Stevenson turned to writing romances for money. *Treasure Island*, which was serialized in 1881, was immediately successful when published in book form in 1883. Other historical novels followed, works which the author himself considered potboilers and described as "tushery," but which have remained popular with readers. Perhaps the best of the adventure tales was *Kidnapped*, which appeared in the magazine *Young Folks* before being brought out in this first edition in 1886. As a letter to his father (see next item) shows, Stevenson was pleased with *David Balfour*, as the novel originally was named, but uncertain about its conclusion. Indeed, he actually finished the story in another book, *Catriona* (1893).

165. Robert Louis Stevenson. Autograph letter signed to his father, Thomas Stevenson (1818–1887), May 1886.

On the subject of his novel *Kidnapped*, which was published in America as *David Balfour*, Stevenson wrote to his father:

The David problem has today been decided[:] I am to leave the door open for a sequel if the public take to it; and this will save me from butchering a lot of good material to no purpose. . . . I am in great spirits about David, [Sidney] Colvin agreeing with [W. E.] Henley, Fanny [Stevenson's wife] & myself in thinking it far the most human of my labours hitherto. As to whether the long eared British public may take to it, all think it more than doubtful. I wish they would for I could do a second volume with ease and pleasure, and Colvin thinks it sin and folly to throw away David and Alan Breck upon so small a field as this one.

166. Robert Louis Stevenson. *Strange Case of Dr Jekyll and Mr Hyde.* London, 1886.

H. G. Wells would create the term "scientific romances" for his own works of the 1890s; but the genre itself, albeit nameless, was already established and flourishing in the 1880s. Stevenson's tale of a dual personality unleashed by a laboratory experiment was among the most successful examples of the merging of imaginative and analytical modes of literature. Framed as a case history, it would prepare the way for other cases in the later years of the decade, including those narrated by Arthur Conan Doyle's fictional man of medicine, Dr. John Watson.

This is the first English edition, which was preceded by the American one by four days.

167. Robert Louis Stevenson. Autograph manuscript, fair copy of "Envoy."

It is likely that this signed manuscript was written by Stevenson at the request of Eugene Field (1850–1895), the Chicago journalist, who pasted it into his copy of *Underwoods* (1887), the volume in which it was printed as the opening poem. Field's writings for children, which include the poem "Wynken, Blynken, and Nod," were greatly influenced by Stevenson's *A Child's Garden of Verses*.

168. William Ernest Henley (1849–1903). *A Book of Verses*. London, 1888.

Like his friend R. L. Stevenson, with whom he collaborated on four plays issued in the 1880s, William Ernest Henley was a semi-invalid who longed to be a traveler and adventurer; and like his friend Rudyard Kipling, whose genius he was among the first readers in England to discover, he was a poet and Aesthete who reviled poets and Aesthetes, longing instead to be a soldier-warrior.

This volume, Henley's first book of poetry, contained the famous sequence called "In Hospital," a vivid and impressionistic rendering, through innovative verse forms and imagery, of Henley's own sensations while a patient of Dr. Joseph Lister at the Edinburgh Infirmary.

169. William Ernest Henley, ed. *Scots Observer: An Imperial Review.* Edinburgh, 1888–90.

Henley's influence as a brilliant editor was perhaps greater than his impact as a poet. In 1881 he was the guiding spirit behind the *Magazine of Art*, which he revolutionized by including articles on Whistler, Japanese wood-block prints, and contemporary French art. His liberal and catholic Aestheticism contrasted sharply with his political conservatism. When given the opportunity to found his own journal, the *Scots Observer* (subtitled significantly *An Imperial Review*), he devoted considerable space to political matters. In this magazine, which became the *National Observer* in 1890 when both he and it moved to London, Henley attempted to gather together the opponents of Decadence. His talented group of contributors—facetiously called by Max Beerbohm the Henley Regatta—included

J. M. Barrie, Andrew Lang, Kipling, Hardy, and Yeats. The second volume of the *Scots Observer* contains one of Henley's few signed contributions, "Nocturn," a poem reminiscent in mood of Whistler's paintings.

 "The Henley Regatta"

170. Jerome Klapka Jerome (1859–1927). *Three Men in a Boat (To Say Nothing of the Dog)*. Bristol, 1889.

Jerome K. Jerome's ambition was to be a serious dramatist and to produce inspirational plays on Christian themes. But it is for two works of comic, anecdotal narrative that he is remembered: *Three Men on the Bummel* (1900) and especially his earlier venture into the same territory, *Three Men in a Boat*. The latter contained what G. K. Chesterton was later to define as one of the hallmarks of true Cockney humor—jokes about smelly cheese (in this case, about a very large wheel of ripe cheese being transported in the overhead rack of a railway passenger carriage). As well as presenting the reader with a lively cast of human travelers on a holiday jaunt, the novel also introduced the elegantly named Montmorency, the "Dog" of the title, who appears in many of the illustrations by A. Frederics.

171. Sir James Matthew Barrie (1860–1937). *Better Dead*. London, 1888.

Unlike Jerome K. Jerome, whose gifts for dramaturgy were inferior to his talents for comic storytelling, the Scottish-born J. M. Barrie seemed equally comfortable—and equally popular with the public—whether writing stage works or prose works. With the publication in 1888 of *Auld Licht Idylls*, sketches of provincial life in his native land, Barrie became one of the first members of what was later known as the Kailyard School of Scottish literature. His identification with Scotland remained strong despite his move to England in the 1880s. He was also, early in his career, closely allied with writers in W. E. Henley's circle. In 1893 he collaborated with Arthur Conan Doyle on the libretto for a comic opera, *Jane Annie: or, The Good Conduct Prize*, which was produced at the Savoy Theater; upon the death of R. L. Stevenson, he made a rare excursion into verse, publishing an elegiac poem called "Scotland's Lament" (1894).

Better Dead represents one of Barrie's few misfires of the period, an insufficiently amusing satire about a club of murderers dedicated to ridding London of social nuisances—a fantasy that may have been inspired by Ko-Ko's aria in Gilbert and Sullivan's *The Mikado*, "I've Got a Little List." In 1896, when the book was republished in

19.   Sir Arthur Conan Doyle, *The Sign of Four*
(London, 1890), frontispiece (item 173)

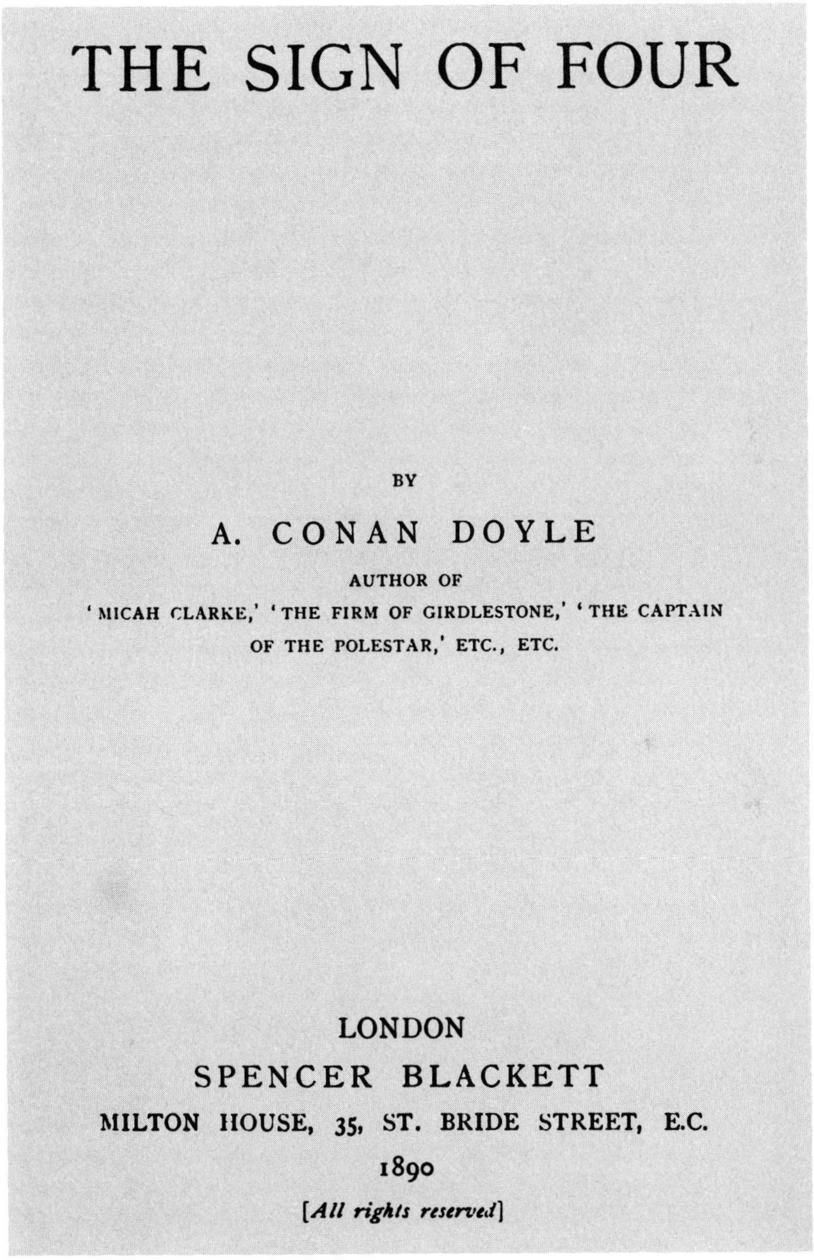

THE SIGN OF FOUR

BY

A. CONAN DOYLE

AUTHOR OF

'MICAH CLARKE,' 'THE FIRM OF GIRDLESTONE,' 'THE CAPTAIN
OF THE POLESTAR,' ETC., ETC.

LONDON
SPENCER BLACKETT
MILTON HOUSE, 35, ST. BRIDE STREET, E.C.

1890

20.   Sir Arthur Conan Doyle, *The Sign of Four*
(London, 1890), title page (item 173)

Scribners' American collected edition of the author's works, Barrie wrote of it in his introduction:

> This juvenile effort is a field of prickles into which none may be advised to penetrate—I made the attempt lately in cold blood and came back shuddering, but I had read enough to have the profoundest reason for declining to tell what the book is about. And yet I have a sentimental interest in 'Better Dead,' for it was my first—published when I had small hope of getting any one to accept the Scotch—and there was a week when I loved to carry it in my pocket and did not think it dead weight. Once I almost saw it find a purchaser. She was a pretty girl and it lay on a bookstall, and she read some pages and smiled, and then retired, and came back and began another chapter. Several times she did this, and I stood in the background trembling with hope and fear. At last she went away without the book, but I am still of opinion that, had it been just a little bit better, she would have bought it.

Although Barrie's first book, this was not his earliest published writing; *Better Dead* was preceded by sketches of Scottish life that appeared in the *St. James's Gazette* and in other magazines.

172. Sir Arthur Conan Doyle (1859–1930). *Micah Clarke: His Statement as Made to His Three Grand-Children, Joseph, Gervas, & Reuben during the Hard Winter of 1734. . . .* London, 1889.

In *A Study in Scarlet*, which was published in Beeton's *Christmas Annual* for 1887 and in book form in 1888, Arthur Conan Doyle created Sherlock Holmes, arguably the best-known fictional character of the late Victorian period, if not of all time. Holmes brought him fame and fortune; but Conan Doyle's true ambition was to write large-scale historical novels. *Micah Clarke*, his first assay at this genre, was "an attempt to show the Puritans in a more favorable light than was customary." The book was surprisingly well received, and its author was encouraged by this response to produce others along the same lines, including *The White Company* (1891), which he considered his best work. Tipped into this copy of *Micah Clarke* is an autograph letter from Conan Doyle to Percy Smith, his host on a visit to Wolverhampton.

173. Sir Arthur Conan Doyle. *The Sign of Four*. London, 1890. See figs. 19 and 20.

In the summer of 1889 J. M. Stoddart, Oscar Wilde's former American publisher and now the representative of *Lippincott's Magazine*, came to London in search of new contributors. Conan Doyle, who had been recommended by James Payn, the editor of the *Corn-*

hill, was invited to meet Stoddart at a dinner at the Langham Hotel. In his autobiography, *Memories and Adventures* (1924), Doyle described the occasion:

> Stoddart . . . proved to be an excellent fellow, and had two others to dinner. They were Gill, a very interesting Irish M. P., and Oscar Wilde, who was already famous as the champion of aestheticism. It was indeed a golden evening for me. Wilde to my surprise had read *Micah Clarke* and was enthusiastic about it. . . .
>
> The result of the evening was that both Wilde and I promised to write books for *Lippincott's Magazine*—Wilde's contribution was *The Picture of Dorian Gray*, a book which is surely upon a high moral plane, while I wrote *The Sign of Four*, in which Holmes made his second appearance.

Lippincott's Magazine, which published the novel as its February 1890 issue, had only a small circulation in England; it was not until the appearance of this first book edition, published at a low price by Spencer Blackett, that *The Sign of Four* became a success.

Rudyard Kipling

174. Rudyard Kipling (1865–1936). *Echoes by Two Writers.* [Lahore, 1884.]

Although Rudyard Kipling is often thought of merely as an imperialist who wrote about India, his early works reveal his close ties to the Aesthetes. His father, John Lockwood Kipling, was an artist and a museum curator; his maternal uncles were the painters Edward Burne-Jones and Edward Poynter. Kipling's juvenile literary efforts appeared first in "The Scribbler" (1879–1881), a manuscript magazine assembled by the children of the Burne-Jones and William Morris families.

Echoes, Kipling's second "book" (it was preceded by *Schoolboy Lyrics,* an 1881 pamphlet), was privately printed by his parents in India. His sister Alice was the co-author; the title refers to the fact that all the poems were written in the style of well-known poets; among those echoed were Browning, Tennyson, Swinburne, Morris, and both Dante Gabriel and Christina Rossetti. This copy is inscribed by Kipling: "W. C. C. d.d. J. R. K. Aug. 1884 / 'And so, like most young poets, in a flush / Of individual life I poured myself / Along the veins of others.'" The book's recipient was W. C. Crofts, the drawing master at the United Services College at Westward Ho!, the school that Kipling attended between 1878 and 1882 and that served as the model for the setting of *Stalky & Co.* (1899).

175. Rudyard Kipling. *Departmental Ditties and Other Verses.* Lahore, [1886]. See fig. 21.

In 1882, at the age of sixteen, Kipling left school in England and

21. Rudyard Kipling, *Departmental Ditties and Other Verses* (Lahore, [1886]), front wrapper in the form of an official dispatch envelope (item 175)

returned to India to take up a post on the *Civil and Military Gazette*, a leading Anglo-Indian newspaper. Many of Kipling's most famous poems and stories appeared in this periodical and its subsidiaries during the next decade. *Departmental Ditties*, printed by the newspaper's press in 1886 in a format imitative of official government orders, was Kipling's first regularly published work and the first to be issued later in England.

176. Rudyard Kipling. *The Story of the Gadsbys: A Tale without a Plot* and *The Phantom Rickshaw and Other Tales*. Allahabad, [1888].

Following the unexpected success of his first book of stories, *Plain Tales from the Hills* (1888), Kipling embarked on the most intensive period of writing of his time in India. Within the same year he published six more volumes of short fiction, all in the Indian Railway Library. *The Story of the Gadsbys* was the second in the series, and *The Phantom Rickshaw* the fifth; the other volumes were *Soldiers Three, Under the Deodars, In Black and White*, and *Wee Willie Winkie*. Each of these volumes had a cover design (done by Kipling's father)—an unusual feature for books meant merely to provide light reading for the traveler, the colonial versions of the English yellowbacks.

177. Spy [Sir Leslie Ward]. *Soldiers Three: Rudyard Kipling*. Color lithograph published in *Vanity Fair*, 7 June 1894. (Lent by Cecil Y. Lang)

This caricature was published while Kipling was at the height of his fame in England but living in Brattleboro, Vermont, with his wife's family. The title alludes to the first of his Indian Railway Library volumes.

178. Sir Henry Rider Haggard (1856–1925). *King Solomon's Mines*. London, 1885.

This novel, the first of Henry Rider Haggard's bestsellers, was the apex of adventure stories of the 1880s. Consciously using *Treasure Island* (1883) as his standard, Haggard tried to top Stevenson by exploiting his own knowledge of the interior of Africa, then a place of mystery to the average English reader. The sales of the book were not harmed by its publisher's advertising it simply as "The Most Amazing Story Ever Written."

179. Sir Henry Rider Haggard. Autograph letter signed to Samuel McClure (1857–1949), 6 December [n.y.].

Haggard wrote this letter to the American publisher Samuel McClure concerning proofs for one of his many novels.

180. Sir Henry Rider Haggard. *She: A History of Adventure*. London, 1887. See fig. 22.

Not everyone was impressed by this exotic story of Queen Ayesha, who had been preserved from death for some three thousand years. Halfway through his reading of the novel, Henry James wrote of it to Robert Louis Stevenson: "It isn't nice that anything so vulgarly brutal should be the thing that succeeds most with the English of today. . . . I am struck with the beastly bloodiness of it . . . such perpetual killing and such perpetual ugliness!"

181. [Andrew Lang and Walter Herries Pollock (1850–1926).] *He: By the Authors of* It, King Solomon's Wives, *and* Bess. London, 1887. See fig. 23.

Haggard dedicated *She* "to Andrew Lang in token of personal regard and of my sincere admiration for his learning and his works." Assisted by his friend W. H. Pollock, editor of the *Saturday Review*, Lang returned the compliment by writing this anonymous parody issued by Haggard's own publisher.

182. Spy [Sir Leslie Ward]. *She: H. Rider Haggard*. Color lithograph published in *Vanity Fair*, 21 May 1887. (Lent by Cecil Y. Lang)

The title of this lithograph refers to Haggard's very successful novel *She*, published in late 1886, which was criticized by *Vanity Fair* in verse:

This is the song of Ayesha
Weird, clever, exciting, full of strange thoughts and true philosophy.
Written by a dead Princess on a Cracked Pot.
Price, six shillings for the lot . . .

183. William Henry Hudson (1841–1922). *The Purple Land That England Lost: Travels and Adventures in the Banda Oriental, South America*. 2 vols. London, 1885.

It is only fitting that one of W. H. Hudson's first admirers and friends in the London literary world was George Gissing. Like Gissing, Hudson was a somewhat gloomy and reclusive character whose work was slow to find an audience. The two shared, moreover, intimate knowledge of life on the edge of poverty and the sense of being displaced persons, inhabiting a hostile environment.

For Hudson the source of his alienation had been his uprooting from the Argentine, where he had spent a happy childhood and adolescence. His passion for the natural world led him to scientific studies, especially in ornithology; his nostalgia for the lost world of his past led him to literary endeavors. His first published book was

22. H. Rider Haggard, *She* (London, 1887), title
page (item 180)

SHE

A HISTORY OF ADVENTURE

BY

H. RIDER HAGGARD

AUTHOR OF

'KING SOLOMON'S MINES' 'DAWN' 'THE WITCH'S HEAD' ETC.

IN EARTH AND SKIE AND SEA
STRANGE THYNGES THER BE

Doggerel couplet from the Sherd of Amenartas

LONDON

LONGMANS, GREEN, AND CO.

1887

23. [Andrew Lang and W. H. Pollock], *He*
(London, 1887), front cover of their parody of
H. Rider Haggard's *She* (item 181)

The Purple Land, a romance of Uruguay, aimed at the reading public that would embrace the exotic subject matter of Kipling's and H. Rider Haggard's tales; but it fared less well than theirs. *Green Mansions* (1904), another expression of Hudson's enduring love for the mysterious landscape of South America, proved to be his only popular work.

 Travel Writers

184. Isabella Lucy Bird [Bishop] (1831–1904). *Unbeaten Tracks in Japan: An Account of Travels on Horseback in the Interior.* 2 vols. New York, 1880.

The movement toward female emancipation found many forms of expression in the 1880s, including a growing body of literature about women travelers and explorers. In some cases the women who left England for exotic places were outspoken feminists; such was true of Lady Florence Douglas Dixie (1857–1905), author of *Across Patagonia* (1880), who had married at the age of eighteen but discovered a greater sense of purpose as a war correspondent in Africa, a big game hunter, and an advocate of sexual equality.

Isabella Bird—although, as a member of an older generation, less radical in her views on the "sex question"—lived a life equally bold and unconventional. In numerous books from the 1850s onward, she chronicled her physically taxing journeys across Canada, the American West, the Sandwich Islands, Australia, and New Zealand, experiences for which she was later honored by being made the first woman Fellow of the Royal Geographical Society in 1892. She did not marry until the age of fifty; after the death of her husband six years later, she turned to the study of medicine and to further travels in the East—Korea, China, and especially India, where she was responsible for founding several hospitals. This work is the first American edition of her two-volume account of an earlier Asian trip, made in 1878.

185. Wilfrid Scawen Blunt (1840–1922). *In Vinculis.* London, 1889.

By birth an aristocrat but by temperament a radical, Wilfrid Blunt was also a poet, explorer, amorist, and "habitual supporter of unpopular causes." In the late 1870s and early 1880s Blunt and his wife, Lady Anne Blunt (Byron's granddaughter), made trips to uncharted areas of the Middle East; on their return to England they collaborated on several pioneering travel books, including *A Pilgrimage to Nejd* (1881) and *The Future of Islam* (1882). Blunt's experiences led him to an interest in Arab political affairs, as well as to the establishment of the finest stable of Arab horses in England. His attention also turned to independence movements in India and in Ireland. He became involved, moreover, with socialism through William Morris (and also became involved with Morris's wife, one of his numerous lovers).

In October 1887 he spoke at a demonstration in Dublin against the Irish landlords; this led to his being sentenced to two months at hard labor for "agitation." Blunt regarded his incarceration as the major event of his political career, writing in his diary that it "deserves to be remembered in Irish history as being the first recorded instance, in all the four hundred years of English oppression, of an Englishman having taken the Celtic Irish side in any conflict, or suffered even the shortest imprisonment for Ireland's sake." While in Galway gaol Blunt wrote *In Vinculis,* a series of sonnets dedicated "to the priests and peasantry of Ireland." The frontispiece of the book is an original etched portrait of Blunt by William Strang.

186. Sir Richard Francis Burton (1821–1890). *A Plain and Literal Translation of the Arabian Nights' Entertainments: Now Entitled the Book of the Thousand Nights and a Night.* . . . 16 vols. Benares [actually printed in Stoke Newington, London], 1885–88.

The original "rebel without a cause," Sir Richard Burton cut a strange figure in Victorian society, which displayed toward him almost as great an antipathy as he felt toward it. As a young man he was sent down from Trinity College, Oxford, where he had shown interest only in challenging fellow students to duels and teaching himself Arabic. From 1842 to 1849 he served with the Indian army, chiefly to learn the languages, customs, and geography of the East, all of which would provide material for four books on India written after his return to England in 1849. His reputation was made by the publication of the *Personal Narrative of a Pilgrimage to El-Medinah and Meccah* (1855–56), an account of how in 1853 he had become one of the few Europeans ever to penetrate the Moslem holy cities, by traveling in disguise as an Indian. The peak of his career as an adventurer was his exploration of equatorial Africa (from 1856 to 1859) to find the source of the Nile, an expedition arranged in part by the Royal Geographical Society. The sensation produced by his reports of this expedition inspired much of the travel literature of the 1880s.

He caused a sensation of another kind with this translation of the *Arabian Nights.* The notes it contained about Eastern sexual customs were considered too obscene for general circulation. It was issued "privately" by the "Kamahastra Society of Benares" in ten volumes

(1885–86) and in six supplemental volumes (1886–88). After Burton's death his dutiful widow, Isabel Arundell, Lady Burton, burned further unpublished translations of Arabic poetry and other "pornography" from his collection.

187. Charles Montagu Doughty (1834–1926). *Travels in Arabia Deserta.* 2 vols. Cambridge, 1888.

Charles Montagu Doughty, a poet, explorer, and notable eccentric, came to the attention of the Victorian public with this record of his adventures from 1870 to 1878 in the Middle East. Although the matter treated in this work was arresting enough in itself, it was Doughty's style that separated this from all other travel literature of the 1880s, a prose style called by some "seventeenth-century," by others "Elizabethan," and by one critic "Chaucerian mixed with Arabic." Like his contemporary Gerard Manley Hopkins (1844–1889), Doughty hoped for a reform of poetic language, away from conventional Victorian idioms to a tougher, more intellectual style, using deliberate archaisms and unexpected rhythms. Despite the fame of *Arabia Deserta*, he turned afterwards almost exclusively to poetry, producing massive patriotic epics in blank verse. These included *The Dawn in Britain* (1906–7), a poem of thirty thousand lines, about the introduction of Christianity into the British Isles in the third century, and *The Cliffs* (1909), which predicted a future invasion of England by Prussian "airships" that would be repelled by the ghosts of English heroes and by elves. The latter work contained the immortal verse, "The Medical Board reported me, as unfit / for further service; and with / a pension, for my wounds, I was discharged." Nevertheless, it is for his travel record of the 1880s, which was reissued in 1921 in an edition prepared by T. E. Lawrence, that Doughty is best remembered.

188. Sir Henry Morton Stanley [John Rowlands] (1841–1904). *In Darkest Africa.* 2 vols. London, 1890.

The author of *How I Found Livingstone* (1872), the story of his search for the explorer that so captured the public's imagination, was often accused of being a self-created hero who embroidered truth for his own purposes. Certainly, Henry Morton Stanley's life represented the triumph of imagination, daring, and resourcefulness over circumstances; he began as a poor workhouse boy, who was later adopted by the man whose name he took, and ended up as a Knight Grand Cross of the Bath, as well as the owner of a gold snuffbox presented by Queen Victoria in gratitude for his services to the nation. These services included his exploration of the Congo (1874–

77), which furthered the partitioning of the region among European nations; his efforts to promote the work of Christian missionaries in Africa; and his expedition from 1887 to 1889 in support of the pro-European Emin Pasha, governor of the Equatorial Province of Egypt, which provided the material for *In Darkest Africa*. With Stanley, the link becomes clear between the supposedly disinterested spirit of adventure and the acquisitive spirit of Empire-building that underlay much of the popularity of travel literature in the 1880s.

189. Robert Bridges (1844–1930). *Prometheus the Firegiver: A Mask*. Oxford: Daniel Press, 1883.

In his first book, *Poems* (1873), Robert Bridges echoed the work of Swinburne. He suppressed the volume soon after publication, however, and from then on kept aloof from contemporary trends. As the possessor of an independent income, Bridges could afford throughout the 1880s to ignore the public's taste; he could also afford the luxury of issuing his books in handsome private editions, some of which were printed at Oxford by his friend Canon C. H. Daniel. *Prometheus the Firegiver* is typical of his work of the 1880s, one of a group of verse dramas which included *Eros and Psyche, Nero*, and *The Feast of Bacchus*. This copy is inscribed to the Catholic poet Coventry Patmore (1823–1896), author of the Victorian best-seller *The Angel in the House* (1854). Bridges remains famous now for another of his friendships, with the poet Gerard Manley Hopkins, whose works he edited (*Poems*, 1918). But Bridges was important in his own right, as the author of *The Testament of Beauty* (1929) and, of course, from 1913 onwards as the poet laureate.

190. Samuel Butler (1835–1902). *The Way of All Flesh*. London, 1903.

Although not published until after the death of its author, *The Way of All Flesh* was in fact a work of the 1880s—one of the most explicit statements of the rage and rebellion against conventional values that, in less articulate form, lay behind all the avant-garde political and artistic movements of the decade. In this autobiographical novel, Samuel Butler declared war upon his own parents in particular, upon the institutions of marriage and the family, upon bourgeois social pretensions, upon Christianity, and upon idealism in general; he did so in the name of freedom for the individual and adherence to the laws of nature. His hero, the naive and obliging young Ernest Pontifex, begins as a dupe of Victorian religion, a sufferer under the repressive sexual morality of the middle classes, and a puppet of his tyrannical father and fanatically pious mother. Through a series of painfully comical mishaps, however, Ernest learns to say no to everything but the promptings of his own nature and thus to be a man.

Friends who read Butler's manuscript in the 1880s considered its attacks upon living people and upon religious doctrine so savage that they persuaded him, for the sake of his own reputation, to leave the work unpublished. When it did at last appear in 1903, it fueled the growing anti-Victorian reaction of the early twentieth century that would culminate in the works of Butler's admirer and fellow satirist Lytton Strachey.

191. Samuel Butler. *Luck or Cunning, as the Main Means of Organic Modification?* London, 1887.

As well as being a composer, classicist, Shakespearian, and novelist, Butler was also a dedicated amateur scientist. After becoming an early convert to the theory of evolution, he broke with his mentor, Charles Darwin, over the details of how the modification of species occurred. Butler throve on controversies and feuds, especially with figures of authority.

192. Samuel Butler. Autograph letter signed to Hyde Clarke, 2 December 1887.

Years after his mentor's death, Butler kept up his scientific dispute with Darwin's family. In this letter he wrote:

As you are good enough to wish to know what I have said about unconscious memory I have told my publisher to send you those of my books that bear upon this subject namely

'Life & Habit'

'Evolution Old & New'

'Unconscious Memory'

'Luck, or Cunning, as the main means of organic Modification?' . . .

As regards my personal quarrel with Mr Charles Darwin I have kept well within the facts—which doubtless is the reason why no answer has ever appeared either from Mr Charles Darwin or any of his sons.

193. Sir [Thomas Henry] Hall Caine (1853–1931). *Recollections of Dante Gabriel Rossetti.* London, 1882.

Hall Caine was a failed architect who turned to journalism for a living in the late 1870s. In 1879 he sent a copy of one of his articles to Dante Gabriel Rossetti. A correspondence between the older painter-poet and his disciple ensued; it led, in 1881, to Caine's installation as Rossetti's housemate in London. Knowing that his carefully contrived friendship with Rossetti would bring him attention, the publicity-hungry Caine wasted no time in writing this book within two months of his hero's death.

An original mounted photograph of Rossetti, by W. and D. Downey, serves as the book's frontispiece.

194. Sir Hall Caine. *The Deemster: A Romance.* 3 vols. London, 1887.

Inspired by Rossetti's own passion for the eccentric and macabre, Caine began writing sensational novels in 1883. *The Shadow of a Crime* (1885) was a moderate commercial success; *The Deemster,* which has been described as an "essay in the prose style as conceived by Victor Hugo," was an overnight best-seller when it appeared in 1887. His later books, such as *The Bondsman* (1890) and *The Eternal City* (1901), were among the most popular novels to have been published up to that time.

Caine's program throughout his work was to advance the cause of "Romance and Idealism," which he saw as an antidote to the realism practiced by others. He expressed his feelings about art in an essay called "The New Watchwords of Fiction" which appeared in the April 1890 issue of the *Contemporary Review:* "the tendency is towards Romance. Not the bare actualities of life 'as it is,' but the glories of life as it might be; not the domination of fact, but of feeling. . . . The cry of the stage of to-day is Romance, the cry of fiction is Romance. . . . The world . . . wants to be lifted up, to be inspired, to be thrilled, to be shown what brave things human nature is capable of at its best."

195. Sir Hall Caine. Autograph letter signed to R. D. Blackmore, 2 January 1888.

To R. D. Blackmore, the author of *Lorna Doone,* Caine wrote: "I'm not at work yet, & it seems probable that before tackling another book I may try my hand at a play. But the drawbacks to that kind of work (even with a stage ready, which is my case) are serious, & the success of 'The Deemster' has brought tempting offers. . . . I hope you'll read 'The D,' for it is my best, & the third volume is more than merely better than anything else of mine."

196. [Edward Carpenter (1844–1929)]. *Towards Democracy.* Part I. Manchester, 1883. See fig. 24.

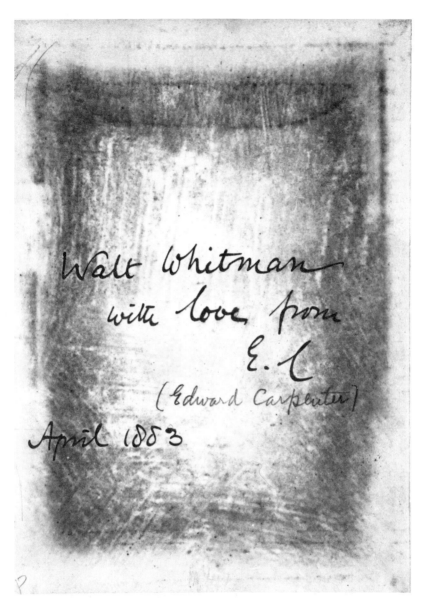

24.   [Edward Carpenter], *Towards Democracy,*
presentation inscription to Walt Whitman (item 196)

The liberating influence of Walt Whitman's democratic vision and notions of poetical diction spread far in England in the 1870s and 1880s, reaching writers as diverse as A. C. Swinburne, Oscar Wilde, and Edward Carpenter, vegetarian, socialist, and advocate of "free-love" (including the variety he called "Homogenic love"). Like the hero of Butler's *The Way of All Flesh,* Carpenter began life conventionally, matriculating at Cambridge and being ordained as a minister. In 1874, however, he relinquished holy orders and dedicated himself to promoting the socialist Utopia of the future, meanwhile writing essays and poems and teaching himself handicrafts (as did William Morris, another convert to politics). On a visit to America in 1877, Carpenter met Walt Whitman, for whom he felt a sort of worship. This copy of Carpenter's most famous work, a visionary poem that would eventually comprise three additional parts and be completed in 1902, is inscribed by the author to Whitman.

197. Harry Buxton Forman (1842–1917), ed. *The Poetical Works of John Keats.* 2d ed. London, 1884. See fig. 25.

The 1880s was a decade of immense growth in literary studies. Amateur scholars such as F. J. Furnivall, university professors such as Edward Dowden, and popularizers such as Austin Dobson, Andrew Lang, and Edmund Gosse all produced important work during this period. Particularly noteworthy were the pioneering textual editions done by H. Buxton Forman, a friend of William Morris and the Rossettis and a civil servant who rose to become comptroller of the Post Office. In 1871 Buxton Forman published *The Shelley Library,* the first modern descriptive bibliography. Specializing in the Romantic poets, he published various editions of Shelley and Keats between 1878 and 1885, including the famous *Letters of John Keats to Fanny Brawne* (1878).

Unknown to his contemporaries was another side of this artful scholar; for with his friend and fellow collector, the notorious Thomas J. Wise (1859–1937), Buxton Forman was responsible for what are now known as the "Wise forgeries," spurious and fabricated editions of leading Victorian writers, including the Brownings, Tennyson, Ruskin, Rossetti, Swinburne, Meredith, and Morris.

This is Buxton Forman's own annotated copy of his first one-volume edition of Keats, with his bookplate.

198. Harry Buxton Forman. Autograph letter signed to J. H. Ingram, 8 November 1883.

Buxton Forman wrote to John H. Ingram: "Here is a Keats prospectus. The book is not issued by subscription. . . . When you

The figure that you here see put
Was for H. Buxton Forman cut.
Amid his household gods to bide
And relics culled from far and wide.
This book is his on whom you look:
For Scott his graving tackle took

And etched the man to watch therein,
That none by guile the book might win.
Then note fur! of great and small
The world holds books enough for all.
Of roughly handling this beware,
And put it in its place with care.

25. Bookplate (depicting its owner) of H. Buxton
Forman, designed by William Bell Scott, in
H. Buxton Forman, ed., *The Poetical Works of Percy
Bysshe Shelley* (London, 1882) (item 197)

see the book & the tremendous list of acknowledgments of indebtedness in the preface, you will understand at a glance where all my few 'author's copies' are gone."

199. Mark Rutherford [William Hale White] (1831–1913). *The Autobiography of Mark Rutherford, Dissenting Minister.* London, 1881.

Like Samuel Butler and Edmund Gosse, William Hale White was the child of religious parents and had lost his faith as an adult. This fictional autobiography, the story of an idealistic minister who abandons the church to work for social progress, has many points in common with Mrs. Humphry Ward's *Robert Elsmere* (1888), which it preceded by seven years, and also much in common with the experiences of actual persons, such as Edward Carpenter. White continued his questioning of Christianity and of the Victorian economic system in his polemic, *The Revolution in Tanner's Lane* (1887). His last novel, *Clara Hopgood* (1896), showed an unexpected sympathy for the plight of fallen women and for England's Jews.

200. William Sharp (1855–1905). *Dante Gabriel Rossetti: A Record and a Study.* London, 1882.

William Sharp's career began much as had Hall Caine's. Born in Scotland, he emigrated to Australia but returned to London in 1878 to become a man of letters. Introduced to Rossetti in 1881 he was, after Caine, the most devoted of the Pre-Raphaelite's younger friends. Like Caine, too, he edited a collection of sonnets by living authors, using the anthology as an entrée into artistic and literary circles.

Sharp's contribution to Rossetti scholarship, this biography relies less on firsthand knowledge than on information from Rossetti's family and earlier friends, whose acquaintance Sharp cultivated. After this book appeared almost simultaneously with Caine's, it was said that whenever a literary figure died "Caine and Sharp would come in with the undertakers."

This copy comes from the library of the American dramatist Henry Bache Smith (1860–1936), who had a fine collection of rare books and manuscripts.

201. William Sharp. *Life of Robert Browning.* London, 1890. (Lent anonymously)

After the favorable reception of his book on Rossetti, Sharp tried his hand at other genres in the 1880s. His first volume of poems, *The Human Inheritance* (1882), showed, as might be expected, his "inheritance" from Rossetti and Swinburne; it was followed by more verse and by a novel called *The Children of To-Morrow* (1889), a "romance" on socialist and Jewish themes. Sharp's steadiest activity remained in the sphere of biography, however, throughout the decade. He published lives of Shelley, Joseph Severn, and Heinrich Heine, and in 1890 he was commissioned to do the first full-length biography of Robert Browning, who had died in December 1889. This copy was presented by Sharp to his friend and rival Hall Caine; throughout the book the recipient marked and commented upon the passages that deal with Rossetti.

In the 1890s Sharp would develop his other identity, by writing under the pseudonym of Fiona Macleod. The Macleod books made him an important part of the Celtic Renaissance, but the secret of their authorship was not made public until after Sharp's death in 1905.

202. Henry S. Salt (1851–1939). *The Life of James Thomson ("B. V."): With a Selection from His Letters and a Study of His Writing.* London, 1889.

Called even by his friends "the poet of pessimism," James Thomson (1834–1882) worked in direct opposition to the optimism of the Victorian age. His life story reads like something by Dickens. His father paralyzed and his mother dead, the young Thomson became an outcast without a family. Eventually he found employment as a "crammer" for army cadets but soon left his post for the literary world in London. At first he relied on hack writing and on a series of odd jobs created for him by the liberal reformer Charles Bradlaugh. Finally, his essays on Blake and Shelley brought him to the notice of George Eliot and William Rossetti; but by this time it was too late. Bad health and penury had driven him to drink, and he lived only two years after the publication in book form of his masterpiece, *The City of Dreadful Night* (1880). In many ways, Thomson anticipated the melancholy spirit of the Aesthetes of the 1880s (and in his brief and tortured career, anticipated the fates of the Decadents of the 1890s). This is the first biography of Thomson, written by his admirer H. S. Salt, an atheist, vegetarian, and Shelley scholar.

203. James Thomson (1834–1882). Autograph letter signed to George Eliot [Mary Ann Evans], 18 June 1874.

Thomson wrote candidly to George Eliot of himself and of his gloomy view of human existence:

> I have no Byronic quarrel with my fellows, whom I find all alike crushed under the iron yoke of Fate; and few of whom I can deem worse than myself, while so many are far better. I certainly have an affectionate and even joyful recognition of the willing labours of those

who have striven to alleviate our lot, tho' I cannot see that all their efforts have availed much against the primal curse of our existence. Has the world been the better or the worse for the life of even such a man as Jesus? I cannot judge, but on the whole I fear considerably the worse. Nonetheless I can love and revere his memory. A physician saves a life, and does well; yet perchance it were better for the patient himself and for others that he now died. But it is not for me to introduce such thoughts to you.

I ventured to send you a copy of the verses (as I ventured to send another to Mr. Carlyle) because I have always read, whether rightly or wrongly, through all the manifold beauty and delightfulness of your works, a character and an intellectual destiny akin to those of that grand and awful Melancholy of Albrecht Dürer which dominates the City of my poem [i.e., "The City of Dreadful Night"].

204. James Thomson. Autograph letter signed to George Eliot [Mary Ann Evans], 20 June 1874.

Thomson, who evidently had been brooding steadily upon the letter he wrote to George Eliot on 18 June 1874, felt driven to send her a further note two days later accounting for the one-sided presentation of life in "The City of Dreadful Night" (which had been published in the *National Reformer* in four issues, beginning on 20 March 1874): "the poem in question was the outcome of much sleepless hypochondria. I am aware that the truth of midnight does not exclude the truth of noonday, tho' one's nature may lead him to dwell in the former rather than in the latter."

205. Sir William Watson (1858–1935). *The Prince's Quest and Other Poems*. London, 1880.

When Hall Caine moved to London in 1881, he made certain that Rossetti saw this first book by his fellow Liverpudlian. *The Prince's Quest* had few reviews and even fewer sales, so William Watson was especially pleased when Rossetti spoke highly of its merits. Watson soon, however, turned against what he called the "latter-day mannerisms" of Rossetti and William Morris; he cultivated instead the use of short lyrics through which he could express his liberal views on politics and literature. His second book, *Epigrams of Art, Life, and Nature* (1884), contained such poems as "The Soudan" and the equally topical "Ireland: Home Rule"; also in the same vein was his bitter attack upon his poetic rivals, "The Battle of the Bards," which appeared in the *Pall Mall Gazette* in 1889. Only reluctantly, when he was at the peak of his fame in the 1890s, did Watson agree to this second issue of *The Prince's Quest* (1892), made up of the original

1880 sheets bound with a new title page and the "Publisher's Note" detailing the book's favorable reception in Rossetti's circle.

206. Sir William Watson. Autograph manuscript signed, "The Church-yard at Chalfont St. Giles."

Watson wrote his poem "The Churchyard at Chalfont St. Giles" while he was on a walking tour with John Lane, his principal publisher in the 1890s. The inscription "Poet Laureate" at the foot of the leaf is not in Watson's hand. It is a misnomer—or a bit of wishful thinking—for, on the deaths of both Tennyson and his successor to the office, Alfred Austin (1835–1913), Watson hoped for but did not receive that coveted appointment.

207. George Bernard Shaw (1856–1950). *Cashel Byron's Profession: A Novel*. London, 1886. See fig. 26.

At the age of twenty George Bernard Shaw left his office job in Dublin and "plunged blindly" into London. For several years he tried to support himself by playing the piano and writing music criticism, all the time working on what he called "the five novels of my nonage." Shaw became an atheist, a vegetarian, and a political radical; allusions to these subjects can be found in the first of these novels to be published, *An Unsocial Socialist*, which appeared in the magazine *To-Day* in 1884 and brought Shaw to the attention of William Morris.

Cashel Byron's Profession, a story about eugenics and boxing, was printed in the same journal in 1885–86 and was then issued from stereotype plates as a "misshapen shilling edition." Shaw later described the reception of the book: "William Archer reviewed it prominently; the Saturday Review, always susceptible in those days to the arts of self-defence, unexpectedly declared it the novel of the age; . . . W. E. Henley wanted to have it dramatized; Stevenson wrote a long letter about it . . . the other papers searched their waste-paper baskets for it and reviewed it . . . and the public preserved its composure and did not seem to care." Although Shaw himself considered Marx, Wagner, and Ibsen to be the principal influences upon his work, R. L. Stevenson described the makeup of *Cashel Byron's Profession* in somewhat different terms:

Charles Reade	1 part
Henry James or some kindred author, badly assimilated	1 part
Disraeli (perhaps unconscious)	$\frac{1}{2}$ part
Struggling, overlaid original talent	$1\frac{1}{2}$ part
Blooming gaseous folly	1 part

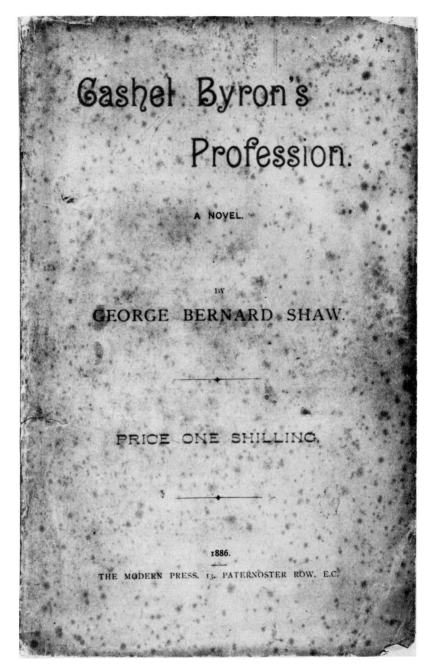

26. George Bernard Shaw, *Cashel Byron's Profession*
(London, 1886), front cover (item 207)

It was not until he began writing plays in the 1890s that Shaw became famous. After 1900 all his novels were republished, except for "one unprinted masterpiece," which the author described as "my Opus 1, which had cost me an unconscionable quantity of paper, and was called, with merciless fitness, *Immaturity*. Part of it had by this time been devoured by mice, though even they had not been able to finish it."

208. George Bernard Shaw. Autograph letter signed to Grant Richards (1872–1948), 22 October 1902.

Shaw wrote to his publisher, Grant Richards, about the augmented edition of *Cashel Byron's Profession*, issued in 1901:

> I have never yet had my attention called to the existence of my own works except by a review. The sale is the old sale to my disciples: I could almost name all the purchasers. I have never seen an advertisement, never met any human being who had ever seen one, never expect to meet one. Cashel Byron is a dead failure in consequence, because all the disciples have cherished it for years; and there has been nothing to tell them that the new edition adds anything to the old.

209. Sir Max Beerbohm. *Caricatures of Twenty-five Gentlemen*. London, 1896.

Although published in 1896, Max Beerbohm's first book of caricatures included many figures of the 1880s, such as Rudyard Kipling and George Moore. George Bernard Shaw, who is depicted in his ubiquitous Jaeger suit, was a favorite target of Beerbohm, who continued to draw him over the next forty years.

210. William Butler Yeats (1865–1939). *Fairy and Folk Tales of the Irish Peasantry*. Edited and Selected by W. B. Yeats. London, 1888.

The 1880s saw a rise of interest in three separate phenomena that converged in the early work of W. B. Yeats: an obsession with investigations into the occult which led serious writers, such as William James and Havelock Ellis, to create the Society for Psychical Research and to contribute to its volume of data, *Phantasms of the Living* (1886); a new curiosity about folk materials and fairy tales, which produced both scholarly collections and the widely popular retellings of Andrew Lang, Joseph Jacobs, and others; and a growing patriotic spirit among Irish writers which encouraged them to mine specifically their Celtic heritage, as did Lady Wilde (mother of Oscar Wilde) in her two-volume *Ancient Legends, Mystic Charms, and Superstitions of Ireland* (1887).

The same year in which this collection by Yeats appeared also saw the publication of an influential anthology, *Poems and Ballads of Young Ireland* (1888), which was unofficially edited by Yeats and included contributions by Katharine Tynan, Douglas Hyde (who was also a contributor to *Fairy and Folk Tales*), T. W. Rolleston, and Yeats himself.

211. William Butler Yeats. *The Wanderings of Oisin and Other Poems.* London, 1889.

After meeting Yeats at W. E. Henley's house and finding the younger poet congenial—even though Yeats's shoes were "a little too yellow"—Oscar Wilde wrote the following unsigned review of *The Wanderings of Oisin:*

> Now and then . . . one comes across a volume that is so far above the average that one can hardly resist the fascinating temptation of recklessly prophesying a fine future for its author. Such a volume Mr. Yeats's *Wanderings of Oisin* certainly is. Here we find nobility of treatment and nobility of subject matter, delicacy of poetic instinct, and richness of imaginative resource. Unequal and uneven much of the work must be admitted to be. Mr. Yeats does not try to 'out-baby' Wordsworth, we are glad to say, but he occasionally succeeds in 'out-glittering' Keats, and here and there in his book we come across strange crudities and irritating conceits. But when he is at his best he is very good.

The review appeared in the *Pall Mall Gazette* of 12 July 1889.

212. William Butler Yeats. Autograph manuscript signed, "When You Are Old."

Yeats's well-known poem "When You Are Old" was written in late 1891. It was first published in *The Countess Kathleen and Various Legends and Lyrics* (1892), his second volume of original poems. From the printed address and telephone number it is apparent that this fair copy was transcribed sometime after 1910.

213. Katharine Tynan [Hinkson] (1861–1931). *Ballads and Lyrics.* London, 1891. (Lent anonymously)

Katharine Tynan, who was associated with Yeats and a contributor to his anthology called *Poems and Ballads of Young Ireland* (1888), was a link between the Aesthetic movement of the 1880s and the Celtic Renaissance of the 1890s. Her first book, *Louise de la Valliere and Other Poems* (1885), contained several monologues in the style of Browning, as well as lyrics dealing with paintings by Burne-Jones and William Holman Hunt. As its title indicated, *Shamrocks,* which followed in 1887, had more poems of Irish interest; the book was dedicated to William Rossetti and his wife.

This is the author's own annotated copy of her third book, which included her most Celtic poem, "The Children of Lir," an allegory, set in the fairy world, about the history of Ireland. In later years Tynan turned to writing novels for a living. In these, as well as in her poems, she demonstrated her ambivalent, middle-class social and political views. She was a supporter of women's suffrage but remained a moderate on the independence of Ireland, referring to the 1917 Easter uprising not as a revolution but as a "rebellion" against English authority.

214. Katharine Tynan [Hinkson]. Autograph letter signed to an unidentified recipient, 29 June 1892.

Referring to Wilfrid Scawen Blunt's earlier imprisonment for Irish political activities, Tynan wrote: "I send by this mail a letter on Mr. Wilfrid Blunt. I hope it will please you. I will try to get tomorrow in Dublin a picture of him in his prison-dress which I shall send you."

WOMEN AND

THE WOMAN QUESTION

 Olive Schreiner and Feminist Debate

215. Ralph Iron [Olive Schreiner, later Olive Cronwright Schreiner] (1855–1920). *The Story of an African Farm: A Novel.* 2 vols. London, 1883. (Lent anonymously)

For the ordinary Victorian novel reader, the feminist movement began in earnest with the publication of Olive Schreiner's *The Story of an African Farm*, an outpouring of passion, anger, and hope, all stimulated by the subject of relations between the sexes. The wide circulation of the book, which helped to create the semi-imaginary figure of the New Woman in the popular press and, more important, which stirred so many actual women to rebel against their lot, was a surprise to both its publisher and its author. Olive Schreiner, a governess leading a life of drudgery in an isolated Boer household, had written her novel (then titled *Thorn Kloof*) in the late 1870s; manuscript in hand, she had left South Africa for London in 1881. As her husband and first biographer, Samuel Cronwright Schreiner, later reported, "she began her attempts to get *The Story of an African Farm* published, but it was rejected by one publisher after another. She was almost in despair when Chapman and Hall accepted it, acting on the advice of their 'reader,' George Meredith. . . . The first edition, a small one in two volumes, was published late in January, 1883, and was soon sold out." From 1881 to 1889 Schreiner remained in England, where she formed friendships with Eleanor Marx-Aveling, Edward Carpenter, and other prominent socialists and also became involved with Havelock Ellis (1859–1939), the sex researcher, in an intimate association which he documented as part of his studies.

216. Olive Schreiner. *Dreams*. London, 1891. See fig. 27.

Like William Morris's dream visions and Oscar Wilde's fairy tales, Schreiner's fantasies used the frame of romance as an aid in the criticism of contemporary society. These allegories, although also concerned with such issues as labor, religion, and the English class system, dealt chiefly with the unsatisfactory relations between men and women. Through the medium of "dreams," Schreiner was able to create her own picture of the Heaven of the Future—someday to be realized on earth—a world without sexual strife, populated by androgynous beings. As she wrote in the final utopian fantasy, "The Sunlight Lay across My Bed,"

> far off on a solitary peak I saw a lonely figure standing. Whether it were man or woman I could not tell; for partly it seemed the figure of a woman, but its limbs were the mighty limbs of a man. I asked God whether it was man or woman.
>
> God said, "In the least Heaven sex reigns supreme; in the higher it is not noticed; but in the highest it does not exist."

217. *Westminster Review*, issues for May and September 1887.

The public debate over the roles, rights, and responsibilities of women was carried on most vigorously in periodicals such as the *Nineteenth Century* (edited throughout the 1880s by James Knowles) and the *Westminster Review*, aimed at serious middle-class readers. The *Westminster Review* proved especially receptive to the points of view of advanced social theorists and reformers—not a surprising fact, given the journal's history; J. S. Mill, later author of *On the Subjection of Women*, had been editor from 1836–40, and in the 1850s George Eliot had unofficially set its policy, with John Chapman as titular editor. In the 1880s the *Westminster Review* gave to the public such controversial articles as "The Woman Question—from a Socialist Point of View" by Eleanor Marx and Edward Aveling, "The Changing Status of Women" by Havelock Ellis, and "Marriage" (a critical examination of the institution) by Mona Caird (1858–1932), as well as the two anonymous contributions in the May and September 1887 issues: "The Emancipation of Women" and "The Law in Relation to Women."

218. Eliza Lynn Linton (1822–1898), Mrs. [Mary Augusta] Humphry Ward (1851–1920), et al. "An Appeal against Female Suffrage," *Nineteenth Century*, June 1889.

"An Appeal against Female Suffrage," protesting against the organized movement to gain the vote, was signed by a long list of prominent women, including Mrs. Leslie Stephen, Mrs. Lawrence

27.   [Olive Schreiner], *Dreams* (London, 1890),
front cover (item 216)

Alma-Tadema, and Mrs. Matthew Arnold. As Emily Davies (a founder of Girton College and a suffragist) remarked at the time, however, most of these were "not distinguished women, but wives of distinguished men." Among the few exceptions were the chief drafter of the "Appeal," Mrs. Humphry Ward, and the novelist Eliza Lynn Linton, famous for her advocacy of the "womanly woman" in her collection of essays, *The Girl of the Period* (1883). The "Appeal," when published in the *Nineteenth Century*, was accompanied by the following request: "that such ladies . . . as agree with it will be kind enough to sign the opposite page and return it, *when detached*, to the EDITOR of this Review." In this copy the "opposite page" is no longer present.

219. Millicent Garrett Fawcett (1847–1929). "Women and Representative Government," *Nineteenth Century*, August 1883.

Unlike the signers of "An Appeal against Female Suffrage," Millicent Fawcett was no mere wife of a distinguished man; rather, she was in her own right one of the most distinguished figures of the age. Although she would go on to ever greater honors, becoming president (1897–1918) of the National Union of Women's Suffrage Societies and being made a Dame of the British Empire (1925), in the 1880s she was already an unofficial leader of the political wing of the feminist movement. In her 1883 article on "Women and Representative Government," typical of her writings of the 1880s, she addressed the politicians among her readers with a direct and simple message, just as a bill in favor of "further extension of the principle of household suffrage" was due to come before the House of Commons: "what the advocates of a real representation of the people want to make sure of, is to remind the orators who make use of these telling phrases, that the human race consists of women as well as of men."

220. Dr. Sophia Louisa Jex-Blake (1840–1912). "Medical Women," *Nineteenth Century*, November 1887.

Sophia Jex-Blake broke with precedent and ignored prejudices on her way to becoming, in the 1870s, one of the first female physicians in the British Isles (Virginia Woolf later would celebrate her memory in *Three Guineas*). In 1874 she founded the London School of Medicine for Women. Her 1887 article for the *Nineteenth Century* provides a useful review of the position of women in medicine in the 1880s, a decade in which scientific training for men had already become widely accepted:

> The progress, then, of the last ten years as regards education and examination may now be summed up. Instead of one examining board

we have no less than seven thrown open to women . . . but the English Colleges of Physicians and Surgeons still remain closed, as also four out of the five English Universities, and all the Scottish Universities, as well as Trinity College, Dublin. . . .

Instead of a single medical school for women we now have three. . . . The number of registered medical women in 1877 was but nine; at the beginning of 1887 the number who had attained registration was fifty-four, and some additional names have since been entered.

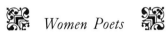 *Women Poets*

221. Mathilde Blind (1841–1896). *George Eliot*. 1st American ed. Boston, 1883.

The daughter of German political refugees, Mathilde Blind was an ambitious writer whose works often explored the problems of her time. *The Heather on Fire* (1886) dealt with the "eviction of the Scottish peasantry," and her most successful poem, *The Ascent of Man* (1889), was an epic on Darwinism. Vernon Lee described Blind as "an ugly, coarse, evidently amiable woman, extremely like Ouida." She was at one point engaged to the American writer Joaquin Miller and, if contemporary gossip can be believed, was more than willing to marry Swinburne.

Blind's *George Eliot*, the first biography of the novelist, was part of the Eminent Women Series edited by John H. Ingram. The series was almost a roster of woman authors with advanced views; among the other volumes were Blind's biography of Madame Roland, *Emily Bronte* by Mary Robinson, and *Mrs. Shelley* by Lucy Madox Rossetti (the daughter of Ford Madox Brown who married William Rossetti and became the mother of two anarchist girls).

222. Mathilde Blind. Autograph letter signed to John H. Ingram, [1885].

Blind, who already had quarreled with her editor, John H. Ingram, over the length of her biography of Madame Roland (published in 1886), wrote him: "I was surprised on receipt of your note asking me to curtail Mme Roland, more especially as in a letter (which I have kept) dated 20 July 1883 you especially requested me to make the life longer than that of George Eliot."

223. Michael Field [Katherine Bradley (1846–1914) and Edith Cooper (1862–1913)]. *Canute the Great and The Cup of Water*. London, 1887.

These two sapphist poets, an aunt and a niece who published under a single male pseudonym, were much admired for their carefully researched historical dramas, none of which was ever performed on a stage. *Canute the Great and The Cup of Water* was the second Michael Field book; it had been preceded by *Callirrhoe and Fair Rosamund* (1884) and by two other volumes issued under the names of Arran and Isla Leigh. The plot of the second play in this book, *The Cup of Water*, was based on a prose sketch by Dante Gabriel Rossetti first published in that author's *Collected Works* (1886). Browning, Meredith, and Ruskin were among the literary folk who became friendly with this unusual couple, for whom, as Sir William Rothenstein later said, "life, which from the first had been given a second place to the practice of literature, lost daily its hold and reality."

224. Michael Field [Katherine Bradley and Edith Cooper]. Autograph letter signed to Theodore Watts-Dunton (1832–1914), 12 November 1887. (Lent anonymously)

When he received this letter Theodore Watts-Dunton, Rossetti's friend and Swinburne's caretaker, had already praised *Canute the Great and The Cup of Water* in the columns of the *Athenaeum;* but he did not yet know that Michael Field was a pseudonym. As though they were one individual, Bradley and Cooper wrote to him concerning another notice of their book:

> It has given me pain and astonishment to find in a review of my new vol. in today's *Spectator* that the writer, after alluding to Rossetti's genius as chiefly for 'the diagnosis of disease' goes on to speak of the plot of *The Cup of Water* as worthy of him. I assumed that every body in the literary world had read Rossetti's argument & would see what I meant when I said I had 'modified it for dramatics.' I have written to the *Spectator* . . . stating that I am responsible for everything in plot & treatment that appears offensive to my critic. Rossetti's King is as 'blameless' as King Arthur.

Not only did the authors conceal, in this letter, their true identities, but also their true address; the return address given was that of their publisher, George Bell.

225. [Agnes] Mary F. Robinson (1857–1944). *Lyrics.* London, 1891.

After studying Greek literature at University College, London, Mary Robinson produced her first volume of verse, *A Handful of Honeysuckle* (1878), and promptly attracted the attention of Browning and the Rossettis. She was soon drawn into the inner circle of the later Pre-Raphaelites, about whom she wrote in a number of English and French periodicals. For several years in the mid-1880s she was, albeit against her family's wishes, the inseparable companion of Vernon Lee, who suffered a mental and physical breakdown in 1887 when Robinson announced her engagement to James Darmesteter, the editor of *La Revue de Paris*. After her marriage to Darmesteter in 1888 she lived mostly in Paris, where she served as a cross-channel link between the most advanced intellectuals. After Darmesteter's death she married Emile Duclaux, director of the Pasteur Institute, in 1901.

Lyrics was the first selection from Robinson's poetry, an attractive volume in Unwin's Cameo Series; other authors in the series included Yeats, Mathilde Blind, William Watson, and Ibsen. The frontispiece reproduces a painting by Botticelli, one of the favorite Renaissance artists of the Aesthetes. Many of the book's poems refer to other pictures, by artists such as Rossetti, G. F. Watts, and Burne-Jones.

226. [Agnes] Mary F. Robinson. *Arden: A Novel*. 2 vols. bound as 1 vol. London, 1883.

Arden, Mary Robinson's first and only novel, is the story of a young woman artist and her adventures in Italy. John Addington Symonds praised the book, but Edmund Gosse, reviewing it in the *Spectator*, expressed concern about its "indelicacies." Like other multivolume novels that were not immediately successful, *Arden* was remaindered, with the unsold sheets being bound up in one volume for sale at a reduced price to the circulating libraries.

227. Christina Georgina Rossetti (1830–1894). *A Pageant and Other Poems*. London, 1881.

After Elizabeth Barrett Browning, the most respected woman poet in Victorian England was probably Christina Rossetti. She contributed to the Pre-Raphaelite magazine, the *Germ*, in 1850 and continued afterwards to work in close association with her brothers, Dante Gabriel and William Michael Rossetti. Her most famous book, known particularly for its title poem, was *Goblin Market and Other Poems* (1862); it was illustrated by Dante Gabriel Rossetti, who also designed the binding of *A Pageant and Other Poems*, a miscellaneous collection. Before 1880 she experimented with a variety of forms, including lyrics for children and short prose sketches, but most of her work of the 1880s was confined to religious meditations in verse.

228. Christina Georgina Rossetti. *Time Flies: A Reading Diary*. London, 1885.

A devout Anglican, Rossetti wrote a number of religious works that are now neglected. *Time Flies* is a devotional calendar with occasional poems, one of a number of her books published by the Society for Promoting Christian Knowledge. Rossetti was in general conservative in her beliefs; but like her brother William (an atheist whose children became anarchists), she sometimes supported advanced views as well. To Augusta Webster, another poet of the 1880s, she wrote: "if female rights are sure to be overborne for lack of female voting influence, then I feel disposed . . . to assert that female *M.P.*'s are only right and reasonable. Also I take exceptions at the exclusion of married women from the suffrage—for who so apt as mothers— . . . to protect the interests of themselves and of their offspring?"

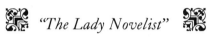 *"The Lady Novelist"*

229. Margaret Oliphant [née Wilson] (1828–1897). *Old Lady Mary: A Story of the Seen and the Unseen*. London, 1884.

Like the novelist Frances Trollope (1780–1863), Margaret Oliphant was a "scribbling" woman who used popular fiction as a means of support for her fatherless, sickly, and otherwise destitute children (her cousin Francis Oliphant, a designer of stained glass whom she had married in 1852, had died at the age of forty-one). She published over 120 books and was a mainstay of *Blackwood's Magazine*. Her specialities were local color, particularly in her stories of Scotland, and tales of the supernatural. Into the latter category fell *Old Lady Mary*, as did another work published two years earlier, *A Little Pilgrim in the Unseen* (1882). Public interest in the "unseen" ran extraordinarily high in the 1880s, especially after the founding in 1882 of the Society for Psychical Research.

230. Margaret Oliphant. Autograph letter signed to R. D. Blackmore, 10 August 1882.

In this letter Mrs. Oliphant, who was usually engaged in several literary projects at once, wrote to a fellow novelist, R. D. Blackmore, to enlist his aid in support of local color:

> I hope you will remember me sufficiently to warrant me in asking you whether you would be disposed to help in a little bit of literary work which I have been the means of suggesting to the Messrs. Longman for a new magazine. . . . It occurred to me some time ago . . . that a series of papers upon the English peasant would be a good one . . . with actual details as to his living, his manners, his work, in short all about him. . . . I promised to write to you and ask if you would contribute one or more papers upon the country folk of your own

country of whom you have given us so many delightful specimens in fiction—would you be disposed to do so? I should myself undertake some little elucidation of my countrymen.

231. Mrs. Humphry Ward [née Mary Augusta Arnold]. *Robert Elsmere.* 3 vols. London, 1888.

The niece of Matthew Arnold and the wife of an Oxford tutor, Mrs. Humphry Ward spent her life in a world of intellectual accomplishments and high moral seriousness. The concerns of her earliest novels were religious. *Robert Elsmere* was the story of a man whose faith in Christianity had been shaken by science, but whose purpose in life was regained through his dedication to social causes. The novel, which mirrored the spiritual pattern experienced by many of the author's contemporaries in the 1880s, became a huge popular success.

In her works from the 1890s onward, however, she turned increasingly to questions involving the lot and destiny of women. Like many members of her generation, she was technically a feminist, believing in the importance of educating women and helping them to become active and responsible participants in society; but she was also a confirmed opponent of the movement to give them the vote. Indeed, she was one of the framers of the widely circulated "An Appeal against Female Suffrage" (1889).

232. Photograph of Mrs. Humphry Ward and Henry James. Platinum print, ca. 1906–10.

The friendship between Henry James, the great American novelist, and Mrs. Humphry Ward, the greatly popular English novelist, began in the mid-1880s and continued through most of their lives. After the enormous financial success of *Robert Elsmere* (1888), James—who, in their early correspondence, would sometimes say, "Let me . . . insist on one or two points in which I should have liked your story to be a little different"—addressed her with less condescension. This photograph was probably taken at Lamb House, James's residence in Rye.

233. Charlotte Mary Yonge (1823–1901). *Lady Hester: or Ursula's Narrative, and the Danvers Papers.* Reprint ed. London, 1889.

The sensational nature of Charlotte Yonge's tale *Lady Hester,* which featured characters with names such as Torwood and Jaquetta, may be judged from the melodramatic postures of the figures in its illustrated frontispiece and from the presence of not one, but two, subtitles.

Yonge had a large and loyal following throughout the 1880s,

although none of her later works equaled the success of *The Heir of Redclyffe* (1853). Her historical romances and "improving" literature of Christian devotion were enjoyed by readers as diverse as Charles Kingsley, William Morris, John Keble, D. G. Rossetti, and by her friends Christabel Coleridge and Mrs. Humphry Ward.

This copy is a reprint edition; *Lady Hester* was first published in 1874.

234. Charlotte Mary Yonge. *Womankind*. 2d American ed. New York, 1890.

Charlotte Yonge's *Womankind* was a work of nonfiction meant to be a guide to proper conduct in all phases of a woman's life from, as the chapter headings indicate, "Nursery Training" to "Old Age." The advice was given from the viewpoint of someone who, even at this late date, still asserted unapologetically that "I have no hesitation in declaring my full belief in the inferiority of woman . . . woman was created as a help meet to man."

This book and the copy of *Lady Hester* both bear the inscription "With the compliments of the author, 1901," probably not written by Yonge herself.

THE THEATER

Gilbert and Sullivan

235. Ape [Carlo Pellegrini]. *English Music: Arthur Sullivan.* Color lithograph, published in *Vanity Fair,* 14 March 1874. (Lent by Cecil Y. Lang)

This lithograph shows Arthur Sullivan exactly one year before he began his triumphant partnership with W. S. Gilbert. Apart from the modest success of *Cox and Box* (1867), his reputation in 1874 rested on the fame of his serious compositions, as well as on his patronage by members of the royal family.

236. Spy [Sir Leslie Ward]. *Patience: William Schwenck Gilbert.* Color lithograph, published in *Vanity Fair,* 21 May 1881. (Lent by Cecil Y. Lang)

To G. K. Chesterton, looking backward in 1930, W. S. Gilbert seemed not merely the great conscious satirist of the late Victorian age but also the unconscious embodiment of its spirit:

Gilbert had no particular positive philosophy to support . . . [his] admirable negative criticism. . . .

This relative lack of moral conviction did mark Gilbert as a satirist, and did to some extent mark all his epoch as an epoch. . . . The original forces that had sustained the hope and energy of the nineteenth century were no longer at their strongest for the rising generation. . . . The typical satire of this period remained what Gilbert himself loved to preserve it, an airy, artistic, detached and almost dehumanized thing; not unallied to the contemporary cult of art for art's sake. Gilbert was fighting against a hundred follies and illogicalities; but he was not fighting for anything, and his age as a whole was no longer certain for what it was fighting.

237. Sir William Schwenck Gilbert (1836–1911) and Sir Arthur Sullivan (1842–1900). *Patience; or Bunthorne's Bride!* New York, 1881.

> *Though the Philistines may jostle, you will*
> *rank as an apostle in the high aesthetic band,*
> *If you walk down Piccadilly with a poppy*
> *or a lily in your medieval hand.*

With his confession that he is "*not* fond of uttering platitudes / In stained-glass attitudes," Reginald Bunthorne, a "fleshly poet," drops his pose and tells the middle-class audience what it wants to hear about the disciples of Aestheticism—that they are shams, not to be taken seriously.

Gilbert and Sullivan's comic opera, which, after first opening at the Opera Comique, was used to inaugurate the new Savoy Theater in October 1881, became the most enduring of all satires of the Aesthetic movement in general and of Oscar Wilde in particular. Richard D'Oyly Carte capitalized upon the public identification of Wilde with *Patience*, paying him to lecture in American cities in which the work was having its premiere in 1882. But Wilde, instead of allowing himself to be exploited, managed to impress with the seriousness of his doctrine of the love of "art for its own sake" the very crowds who had expected to laugh at him.

This copy of *Patience* may be a first American edition.

238. Sir W. S. Gilbert and Sir Arthur Sullivan. *The Mikado; or The Town of Titipu*. New York, 1885.

The late Victorian craze for things Japanese—perhaps the most lasting effect of the Aesthetic movement on middle-class taste—was touched off by the International Exhibition of 1862, held in South Kensington, where many Londoners were introduced to the porcelains, fans, and lacquered furniture of the Orient. Furnishings in the Japanese style became widely available to the public in 1875 when Arthur Lasenby Liberty opened his shop on Regent Street, where it stands today. Gilbert and Sullivan added their own contribution to the flood of *japonisme* with *The Mikado*. Produced by Richard D'Oyly Carte, this comic opera received its first performance at the Savoy Theater, London, on 14 March 1885 and its American premiere in New York on 19 August 1885. Although it was set in Japan, its objects of satire were all distinctly Victorian, including such targets as "that singular anomaly, the lady novelist."

This is the first American edition of the libretto.

239. W. S. Gilbert. Autograph letter signed to Sir George Henschel (1850–1934), 15 September 1893.

Gilbert writes to the famous conductor George Henschel, who led the Boston Symphony from 1881 to 1884, about a young singer: "I think Sullivan has written some of her music unnecessarily high. . . . she has some very high solo declamation to do which surely might be transposed without injury to the work. I mean to take an opportunity of suggesting this to him—quite prepared to swallow the inevitable snubbing which it will produce. He *snubs— but he usually carries out my suggestions,* nevertheless."

 Actors

240. Ellen Terry (1847–1928) and Henry Irving (1838–1905) in *Romeo and Juliet*. Wood engraving published in the *Illustrated London News*, 18 March 1882. See fig. 28.

241. *Miss Ellen Terry*. Photogravure portrait published in W. Eden, comp. *The Stage in the Year 1900: A Souvenir*. London, 1901.

242. Sarah Bernhardt (1844–1923). Photograph made ca. 1910 by William E. Gray, London, reproducing an earlier print made privately. The actress posed in the coffin in which she sometimes slept.

The London stage of the 1880s was dominated by a star system that gave prominence and power to a handful of actors, male and female. Some of these, such as Lily Langtry, exploited their popularity by appearing in dramatically worthless vehicles that were mere excuses for showing their faces to the public. Others, however, took their art more seriously, reviving the classics and working closely with first-rate artists and designers on their productions to achieve visual coherence and beauty. Among the latter were the actor-manager of the Lyceum Theater Company, Henry Irving; his leading lady, Ellen Terry; and the French actress, Sarah Bernhardt, whose London appearances proved so inspirational to the Aesthetes in particular. All three numbered avant-garde writers, composers, and painters among their intimates—as friends, admirers, lovers, and even spouses. All rose, too, from undistinguished social origins to move in the highest circles of society and, eventually, to be honored by their countries: Irving became, in 1895, the first actor to be knighted; his co-star was made Dame Ellen Terry in 1925; Bernhardt received the recognition of the Legion d'Honneur in 1911.

The 1880s saw the beginning of a new appreciation of stagecraft, as one of the fine arts, on the part of the middle classes, who had puritanically avoided the pollution of contact with the theater for much of the nineteenth century. (This loosening of prejudices, how-

28. Ellen Terry and Henry Irving in *Romeo and Juliet*, wood engraving published in the *Illustrated London News*, 18 March 1882 (item 240)

ever, was slow in filtering down to the lower middle classes, as evidenced by George and Weedon Grossmiths' *The Diary of a Nobody*, published in book form in 1892, in which Mr. Pooter, the City clerk, is appalled to learn that his son takes part in amateur theatricals.) Certainly, the traditional assumption that the theater was a pit of corruption was no longer going unchallenged. On his first tour of America in 1883, Irving was asked by a reporter for his response to the hostility felt by "a large class of people, both intelligent and cultured, who still look upon the stage and stage-plays, even if not downright immoral, as not conducive to any intellectual or moral good." He was alleged to have replied: "Such ideas are due to ignorance. . . . When bigotry and superstition fade, and toleration triumphs, then the work of which the stage is capable will be fairly judged, and there will be no bar to encounter. The lesson of toleration is not for the player alone; the preacher must learn it" (Henry Irving, *Impressions of America* [Boston, 1884]). Indeed, these "players" achieved public acceptance and received adulation before most of their associates in the worlds of literature or painting did. In the 1880s it was the interpretive artists who bridged the gap between the Aesthetes and the Philistines.

 Public Spectacle

243. *Queen Victoria's Jubilee.* Two wood engravings, published in the *Illustrated London News*, 25 June and 2 July 1887.

The greatest theatrical event of the decade did not take place on any stage but in the churches, public edifices, streets, and skies of London. From 21 June to the end of the summer of 1887, spectators were treated to concerts, parades, fireworks, electrical "illuminations" of selected buildings, and a naval regatta along the Thames in honor of Queen Victoria's Jubilee. An occasion that brought together the widest possible range of social classes and professions, it was, in a decade marked by violent controversies and accelerating social change, a celebration of harmony both rare and fleeting.

❦ INDEX OF NAMES ❦

Note: The references are to the catalogue numbers.